THE DRINKING
WATER BOOK

THE DRINKING WATER BOOK

A COMPLETE GUIDE TO SAFE DRINKING WATER

Colin Ingram

Ten Speed Press
Berkeley, California

1☯

Ten Speed Press
P.O. Box 7123
Berkeley, California 94707

Cover design by Nancy Austin
Text design by Victor Ichioka
Typesetting by Ann Flanagan Typography

Library of Congress Cataloging in Publication Data

Ingram, Colin, 1936–
    The drinking water book : a complete guide to safe drinking water
    Colin Ingram.
    200p.   cm.
    Includes bibliographical references.
    ISBN 0-89815-436-7
    1. Drinking water—United States—Contamination.   2. Water
    quality—United States.   I. Title.
RA592.A1I54   1991
613'.3—dc20   91-14714 CIP

First printing, 1991
Printed in the United States of America
    2 3 4 5 – 95 94 93 92

Contents

INTRODUCTION

Does Anyone Know What They're Talking About?

INTRODUCTION

A few years ago I was living in a mountainous rural area of Appalachia, far removed from all obvious sources of pollution. Yet in this pristine region there was an epidemic of cancer among the scattered residents. After much publicity and badgering, the state was forced into investigating the problem. The result was a "gray wash." That's when the investigating body admits there may actually be a problem but announces the results of the investigation over an extended period of time in order to dilute citizen response, and suggests that there are many causes of the problem so that it is hard to take action against any one of them.

But there were definite indications that something in the local environment was contributing to the cancer epidemic. Finally, tiny traces of an herbicide were found in our supposedly pure water supplies—an herbicide that the manufacturer and all of the involved government agencies swore was harmless. This led me on a quest for information about whether or not the chemical was really harmful and if so, what to do about it.

The journey took me to public waterworks, county and state health agencies, testing laboratories, universities, and to the Environmental Protection Agency (EPA). It expanded to include toxicologists and epidemiologists, bottled water companies and manufacturers of water purifiers. It culminated in a five-year research program (with no grants or other assistance to prejudice the results), and the founding of a drinking water research center. This book is one result of that research.

During those five years, I discovered many things that the general public is unaware of. For example:

- Although most public health officials claim that your drinking water is safe, they don't really know if it is safe or not. In fact, no one knows what "safe" is.

- Federal and state standards for drinking water safety are inadequate, covering only a small fraction of the toxic substances that may be in your water.

- Right now, there are known cancer-causing chemicals in essentially every public water supply in the country.

- Water fluoridation does more harm than good.

- Some bottled water is a greater health threat than tap water.

- Some water purifiers for home use add more pollutants to the water than they remove.

- Performance claims by water purifier manufacturers are often biased, misleading or irrelevant.

- The majority of water tests performed for consumers in the United States are bogus, meaningless or unreliable.

- Popular magazines and consumer publications that test or report on water products generally do not have sufficient knowledge of what they are doing to provide consumers with useful information.

This is not to say that there aren't experts in specialized areas of water quality—there are. But very few of them know enough outside their own specialty to help consumers. For example, try asking your local health department officials about the relative merits of different brands of distillers. Or ask a water filter salesperson for data on bacterial growth within filters. Or ask a bottled water dealer about studies that have shown that the plastic from some water bottles can migrate into the water and affect your immune system.

My purpose isn't to criticize these people, who, by and large, are trying to be helpful, but to point out that the consumer has had nowhere to go for the facts about safe drinking water. No one had put it all together to try to make sense out of all the conflicting claims.

The Drinking Water Book does put it all together. It helps you find out if you really need to do something about your drinking water—and what might happen if you don't. It shows you how to avoid bogus tests, scams and unnecessary expenditures. It describes the most cost-effective ways to get better water, including some things you can do without spending a penny. If you decide to buy a purifier, it tells you about all of your options, how to narrow your choices and the best buys available.

The Drinking Water Book includes tips and information you won't find in any other popular source, such as a summary of what is known about health-*giving* water—what kinds of water have been scientifically shown to help maintain and improve your health. While the information in this book is presented in a simple, easy-to-absorb form, it is based on years of extensive research on water quality and on actual testing of products, not just in laboratories but in actual installations in homes.

For many years, American consumers have been faced with frightening headlines about unsafe drinking water, without any real guidelines on what to do about it. This book fills that gap.

CHAPTER 1

Questions And Answers

CHAPTER 1

Why Should I Be Concerned About My Drinking Water?

Q I have heard news stories about toxic substances in drinking water, but I have also heard public health officials claim that there is no danger. Is there really a health threat from drinking tap water?

A In some areas the toxic substances in tap water pose an obvious and serious health threat. In other areas, where the tap water is better, the health threat still exists but is harder to pin down. However, *all* drinking water that is consumed straight from the tap does pose a health threat to some degree.

Q How can there be polluted water in areas with no history of toxic substance use?

A (1) There is no way to know for sure whether toxic substances have been used in a given area, (2) the water may originate from another area where toxic substances have been used, (3) some of the chemicals used to treat water and make it safe are themselves harmful, and (4) water pipes within and outside of the house can also deposit pollutants into the water.

(For more information on the toxic substances found in water supplies, see Chapters 2 and 3.)

Who Is Responsible For Safe Drinking Water?

Q Who is responsible for insuring that our water is safe?

A A combination of federal, state and local government agencies, and water utility companies.

Q If tap water is unsafe for drinking, why does the government allow it?

A Because it would cost a lot of money to make it safe; because politicians support industries that pollute water; and because water utility companies are resisting their responsibility to make it safer.

Q That's crazy. Isn't the purpose of water utilities to provide safe water?

A Yes, but they are oriented toward eliminating immediate health threats from water (like harmful bacteria); they generally try to avoid the responsibility for eliminating the tiny amounts of chemicals that are harmful only after years of ingestion.

Q Why do water utilities want to avoid this responsibility?

A Accepting this responsibility would mean changing traditional methods of treating water for public consumption. It would mean adding a whole new dimension to water treatment.

Q I hear that industry is still polluting water. Why doesn't the government force industry to stop discharging pollutants into water supplies?

A It would cost industry a great deal of money to stop discharging pollutants and, rather than finding solutions to the problem, industry pressures the government to allow the pollution to continue.

Q So, in spite of the taxes I pay, it sounds like *I* have to be responsible for the safety of my drinking water.

A Partially. The water utilities generally do a good job of providing water that is free of those pollutants that will make you sick immediately. What they don't do is remove those pollutants that can harm you over a period of time.

(For more information on government water policies and regulations, see Chapter 3.)

Should I Have My Water Tested?

Q How can I find out what is actually in my tap water?

A If your water is from a water utility company, you should be able to get a copy of test reports that show whether or not certain toxic substances are in the water. While these reports are helpful, they do *not* include a large number of other toxic substances that may be in the water.

Q If I want to get a more comprehensive test of my water, will my local health agency pay for it?

A In general, no, unless one or more persons in your family have become sick and your doctor suspects water is the cause.

Q How do I get a comprehensive test of my water?

A You will have to pay for testing by a private laboratory. While most test labs charge very high prices, there are a few automated labs that offer low-cost, comprehensive testing.

Q So should I have my tap water tested?

A Testing may not be needed, because it is often possible to infer a great deal about your water from information already on hand. But whether it is tested or not, I recommend that you do *not* drink tap water unless necessary.

(For more information on how to find out what's in your water, see Chapter 3.)

What Should I Do About My Drinking Water?

Q What are my options?

A The first thing to do is to stop drinking tap water as soon as possible. Then you have three basic choices: buy bottled water, buy water from a vending machine or water store, or install a water purifier at home. Even if you decide to install a water purifier, start drinking bottled or machine-vended water until it is in place.

Q Which will give me the best-quality drinking water—bottled water, machine-vended water or using a purifier?

A It depends on the particular kind you choose. If you buy the *right* kind of bottled water, its quality will be high; however, some bottled waters are worse than tap water. *Most* machine-vended water is of high quality. Water purifiers vary from extremely good to very bad; some purifiers actually add toxic substances to the water. The effectiveness of a purifier often depends on correctly matching it to your particular water conditions.

Q If I want to drink bottled water, which kind should I buy?

A Buy a well-known, major brand from a store that sells a lot of it. Choose a label that says "drinking water." If that is not available, choose "purified water" or "distilled water" until you can find "drinking water." Do not buy "spring water," "natural spa water," "natural mountain water" or any other label that indicates that the water is from a natural source.

Q But don't natural springs have the purest water?

A Not necessarily. Natural sources are sometimes contaminated by naturally occurring toxic pollutants.

Q If I want to drink machine-vended water, can I choose any machine?

A Choose a popular location where the machine gets a lot of business. Look for a label or seal on the machine that indicates it is inspected by the county or other local health agency. Make sure your containers are clean.

Q What should I know before buying a water purifier?

A That's a more complicated question. Don't buy or rent any water purifier until you have read the sections in this book on purifiers.

(For more information on bottled water and water vending machines, see Chapter 6. For more information on water purifiers, see Chapters 7 through 11.)

Water Pollutants
And The
Risk To Health

CHAPTER 2

What Kinds Of Pollutants Are In Our Water?

Let's begin by dividing all water pollutants into two broad categories: nuisance pollutants and health-threatening pollutants. Nuisance pollutants are those that cause discomfort or inconvenience. They can cause water to taste, smell or look bad, and they can render soap and washing less effective.

Health-threatening pollutants fall into five categories.

The five types of health-threatening water pollutants:
- ◆ **Microorganisms**
- ◆ **Toxic minerals and metals**
- ◆ **Organic chemicals**
- ◆ **Radioactive substances**
- ◆ **Additives**

Microorganisms

Microorganisms include harmful bacteria, viruses and parasites. They can cause such diseases as typhoid, cholera, hepatitis and flu. Bacteria are closely monitored in public water supplies, because they can be dangerous and because their presence is easily detected. Tap water from a public supply is generally free of dangerous concentrations of bacteria because they are killed when chlorine is added. Viruses are very common in water. Recent research has shown that a teaspoon of unpolluted lake water contains over a *billion* viruses. Viruses are much smaller

1 billion viruses per spoonful of unpolluted lake water

than bacteria and harder to detect. Although disinfecting tap water with chlorine probably kills the majority of viruses in the water, no one knows for sure how many remain potent. It is more difficult to test for the presence of viruses in water than it is for bacteria, and most water-testing laboratories do not have the ability to do this. While most waterborne viruses appear to be harmless to humans, some are the cause of cold and flu epidemics. *Harmful viruses can be present in tap water even though a water treatment plant is operating properly.*

The third group of microorganisms commonly found in water is protozoan parasites. The two most common and troublesome of these are called *giardia* and *cryptosporidium*. In water, these parasites occur in the form of hard-shelled cysts. Their hard covering protects them from the chlorine disinfection that kills other microorganisms. Both of these parasites cause mild to severe gastrointestinal symptoms in healthy people. In people with impaired immune systems, they can be life threatening. *Parasites can be present in tap water even though a water treatment plant is operating properly.*

In spite of the effective elimination of bacteria in public water supplies, other microorganisms in the water can be a serious health hazard.

Toxic Minerals

Toxic minerals are the harmful inorganic substances that are found in water supplies (*inorganic* means not derived from plant or animal matter). They include metals as well as common minerals in the form of rock, sand and clay. It's important to distinguish between minerals that are harmful and those that are mere nuisances. The main nuisance minerals are:

- Calcium and magnesium, which cause hardness in water
- Iron and manganese, which cause staining
- Hydrogen sulfide gas, which causes a rotten-egg odor

The minerals in water that are actually harmful to health are:

- Aluminum
- Arsenic
- Asbestos
- Barium
- Cadmium
- Chromium
- Copper
- Fluoride
- Lead
- Mercury
- Nitrate
- Nitrite
- Selenium
- Silver

These toxic minerals are naturally occurring in water and they also enter water from man-made sources. Some of them are more toxic than others. Cadmium, lead and mercury have the greatest toxicity, and even the ingestion of small amounts can cause death. The ingestion of asbestos fibers is known to increase the risk of cancer. These fibers commonly occur in certain kinds of rock formations, especially those known as "serpentine." They are also present in water wherever asbestos-cement (AC) water pipes are used to deliver water to customers (just about everywhere in the United States). In very low level doses, toxic minerals can, over a period of many years, cause disorders of the kidneys, bones, blood and nervous system.

High levels of nitrates and nitrites in water usually occur in agricultural areas where large amounts of fertilizers are used and livestock are raised. High levels of nitrates and nitrites cause "blue baby" disease in infants and intestinal disorders in adults.

Toxic minerals can enter a water supply from naturally occurring sources in surface or ground water; they can come from industrial discharges, runoff from urban and agricultural areas and from the walls of water mains; and they also can come from sources within the home. Metal pipes, joints and plumbing fixtures, especially sink faucets, are frequent sources of toxic mineral pollution.

In general, where high levels of toxic minerals are in a water supply, water treatment plants do a good job of reducing them to safer levels (not to completely safe levels—just to safer levels). The exception to this is asbestos. Most water treatment plants do not currently have the technology to efficiently remove asbestos from water, nor do they regularly test for its presence. Where asbestos-cement pipes are used to deliver water, any cutting, repairing or relocating of these pipes can cause large amounts of asbestos to enter the water. Even changes in water pressure within the pipes can cause high levels of asbestos to enter water. When asbestos does enter a water supply, it is generally undetected, and the consumer has no warning.

Organic Chemicals

Organic chemicals are substances that come directly from, or are manufactured from, plant or animal matter. Plastics, for example, are organic chemicals that are made from petroleum, which originally came from plant and animal matter. There are roughly

100,000 different manufactured, or synthetic, organic chemicals in commercial use today. They include synthetic fertilizers, pesticides, herbicides, paints, fuels, plastics, dyes, flavorings, pharmaceuticals and preservatives, to name a few. Many of these chemicals are toxic, and thousands of them have been found in public water supplies. When synthetic chemicals are found in a water supply, the actual polluting source may be a leaking gasoline tank or factory discharge many miles away, it may be agricultural runoff, herbicide spraying of highways or any of hundreds of legal or illegal sources. Often, pollution of a water supply by synthetic chemicals has no obvious source—yet toxic chemicals are present.

One type of organic chemical is particularly dangerous. Volatile organic chemicals, or VOCs, are absorbed through your skin when you come into contact with water, as in a shower or bath. Further, hot water allows these chemicals to evaporate rapidly, and they are harmful if inhaled. VOCs can be in any tap water, regardless of where you live or what your source of water is. If your tap water should contain significant levels of these kinds of chemicals, they will be a health threat from skin contact with the water even if you don't drink it.

In addition to the organic chemicals that have gotten into water supplies, new and dangerous ones are created in the water itself. Chlorine, which is in essentially all U.S. tap water, combines with organic chemicals to form a category of toxic pollutants called THMs (for trihalomethanes).

Chlorine   Organic Chemicals   THMs

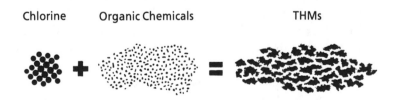

THMs are known carcinogens—substances that increase the risk of getting cancer—and they are present at varying levels in all tap water.

Radioactive Substances

Radioactive substances in water are of two types: radioactive minerals and radioactive gas. Radioactive minerals can be either naturally occurring or man-made. When naturally occurring, their source is typically an area where mining is going on or has gone on in the past. Uranium mining produces radioactive runoff, as you might expect. But other kinds of mines also enable radioactive minerals to enter water supplies. This is because mining exposes rock strata, most of which contains some amount of radioactive ore. Other sources where naturally occurring radioactive minerals can enter water supplies are smelters and coal-fired electrical generating plants.

Man-made sources of radioactive minerals in water are nuclear power plants, nuclear weapons facilities, radioactive materials disposal sites and docks for nuclear-powered ships. An unreported area of radioactive pollution comes from hospitals all over the country, which are allowed to dump low-level radioactive wastes into sewers. Some of these radioactive wastes eventually find their way into water supplies.

If the source of your water is a reservoir, river or mountain runoff that is near or downstream from any mining areas or nuclear facilities, you should pay special attention to finding out the level of radioactivity in your water.

While radioactive minerals in water may present a health hazard in these particular areas, a far more dangerous threat exists in the form of radon. Radon is a colorless, odorless, naturally occurring gas that is the by-product of the decay of radioactive minerals. It is present in all water in minute amounts, and it is especially concentrated in water that has passed through rock strata of granite, shale, phosphate or uranium.

> **Radon is a known cancer-causing agent. When present in household water, it evaporates easily into the air and is inhaled. The effects of radon inhalation are now believed to be more dangerous than those of any other environmental hazard.**

Radon dissipates rapidly when water is exposed to air. Because of this, radon is not a threat from surface water— where the water source is a lake, river or above-ground reservoir.

If water comes from an underground source, radon is still not a threat if the water is aerated (exposed to air) or if it is processed through an open tank during treatment.

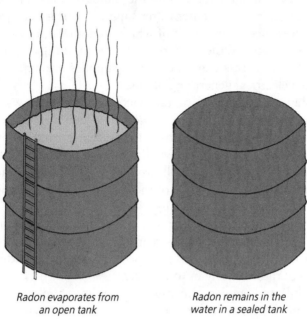

Radon evaporates from
an open tank

Radon remains in the
water in a sealed tank

Radon *is* a threat from ground water that comes into the home *directly* from an underground source—either from a private well or from a public water supply whose source is a well and whose treatment of the water does not include exposure to air. Because radon in water evaporates quickly into air, the primary danger is from inhaling it from the air in a house, not from drinking it. The Environmental Protection Agency estimates that at least 20,000 cases of cancer in the United States each year are caused by radon inhalation.

Although the main radon problem is not, strictly speaking, a water problem, it is such a serious threat that I want to give you a few more details. Radon gas enters a house in two ways: from the soil beneath the house, through cracks in the foundation, etc.; and via the water system. Studies show that where there are high concentrations of radon within the air in a house, *most* of the radon comes through the foundation and not from the water.

Radon concentrations within a house are highest in winter when all windows are shut. The problem is worsened by energy-efficient dwellings that have been tightly sealed to prevent heat loss. Basements have the highest radon concentrations. Also, if radon is in the water, showers, baths and cooking (with hot water) will cause high concentrations of radon in the air.

If radon is in tap water, any areas in a house where the water is exposed to turbulence and/or heat will have high concentrations of radon.

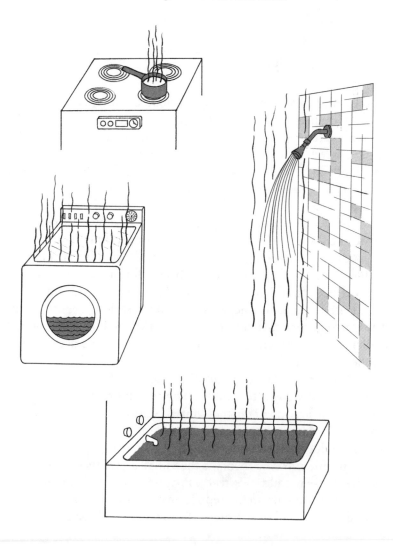

If you live in a ground-level dwelling (as opposed to an upper-story apartment), and if you do nothing else as a result of reading this book, **I urge you to contact your county health department and your local water company and find out if radon is present in your area. If it is, have your house tested for it as soon as possible. If you do have high levels of radon in your house, act to reduce them as soon as possible.** In the Radon Supplement following Chapter 12 I discuss the things you can do to accomplish this.

Additives

 ◆ **Chlorine**
 ◆ **Fluoride**
 ◆ **Flocculents**

Public water treatment plants, from small community systems to larger, urban waterworks, all add things to water. The best-known additive is chlorine. Chlorine is used in almost every public water system in the United States, and it has proved beyond any doubt to be an effective disinfectant. For decades it has been assumed that small amounts of chlorine in drinking water are safe. But convincing evidence, largely unreported to the public, has been accumulating for many years that shows correlations between chlorinated water and the onset of serious diseases (see Appendix B for references). Ingesting small amounts of chlorine, itself *may* pose a long-term health threat. But there is overwhelming evidence that the toxic chemicals formed when chlorine combines with organic chemicals in water *are* a serious health threat. These toxic chemicals are known as THMs and, as I mentioned earlier in this chapter, they are now present to some degree in all public water supplies.

Water fluoridation is another subject that has not been reported very well to the public. The pro-fluoridation and anti-fluoridation argument in the United States has been going on since 1947, when plans to add fluoride to drinking water were first introduced. Does fluoridated water really prevent tooth decay in children? The theory is that small amounts of fluoride in the diet harden children's teeth. Proponents of fluoridation cite studies that show dramatic reductions of tooth decay in children who drink fluoridated water. Opponents of fluoridation cite equally valid studies that show no difference in the dental health of children in fluoridated and nonfluoridated areas.

There are some important facts to remember about water fluoridation. First, fluoride is a potent poison whose level of ingestion must be carefully regulated. The difficulty is that no one knows for sure how much fluoride the average child is receiving. This is because, in addition to water fluoridation, children can ingest fluoride through toothpaste and through the fluoridated water that may be used in canned foods and beverages. In follow-up studies of school programs where children rinsed their mouths with a fluoride solution, many young children were found to be swallowing the rinse instead of spitting it out as the teachers instructed. Also, fluoride is notoriously hard to add to water in precise amounts, and its actual level may vary considerably from day to day. So a "safe" amount of fluoride in water may not be safe when combined with the fluoride ingested from all other sources.

In addition to hardening children's teeth, a side effect of fluoride is that it frequently causes tooth discoloration (a mottling effect, with white and darker spots). More importantly, fluoride is suspected as a factor in the long-term onset of diseases of the bones, including cancer. Significantly, many American communities that had been using fluoridated water stopped doing so once all of the facts became known. And in fact, almost all of the other industrialized countries in the world have rejected water fluoridation, in spite of U.S. pressure for them to initiate it.

For those readers who want to pursue the subject of water fluoridation, I have listed some thought-provoking reference material in Appendix B, which I highly recommend for further reading. Of all the research I have investigated over the years, I have never seen a public program so fraught with errors and misinformation. Based on my research on this subject, **I believe that water fluoridation is one of the most irrational and health-threatening programs ever offered to the American public. I firmly believe the harm from fluoridated drinking water far outweighs the benefit, and I recommend that you and your children do not drink fluoridated water.**

In addition to chlorine, and sometimes fluoride, water treatment plants often add several other substances to water to improve the efficiency of treatment. *Flocculents* are substances that are added to the water to make the particles in it clump together for more efficient removal by filtering. Some of the most

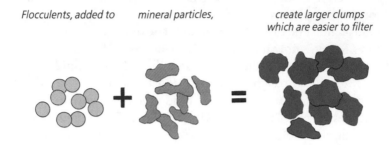

Flocculents, added to   mineral particles,   create larger clumps
                                                    which are easier to filter

commonly used flocculents are called polyelectrolytes. These types of flocculents have been banned for use by several other countries because some of their constituents are known to be mutagenic (causing genetic mutations) and carcinogenic (cancer-causing substances). The Environmental Protection Agency, while classifying some of these flocculents as "probable human carcinogens," still permits their use.

Taste, Smell And Appearance

The taste, smell and appearance of drinking water are normally mere nuisance factors. A brownish-colored water, for example, usually indicates the presence of harmless dirt or iron in the water, and a cloudy appearance may be no more than normal minerals in the water coming out of solution. But there are also many instances when a bad taste or smell, or cloudy water, indicates the presence of harmful pollutants, such as bacteria. In general, if you notice an unusual taste or smell, or a change in the appearance of your tap water, immediately contact your water utility company and don't use the water for any purpose until you are given assurance that the water is safe.

Estimating Overall Health Risks

In the United States, water treatment has concentrated on the elimination of short-term health risks—bacterial or viral infection or acute poisoning from a sudden, large dose of lead or mercury. In this regard it has been fairly successful. Serious waterborne diseases have been mostly eliminated. At the same time, those responsible for water quality have, until recent years, turned a blind eye to the long-term health effects of polluted water.

One of the excuses for not confronting water pollution problems is that pollutants in very tiny amounts are often dismissed as inconsequential. Analogies are created for drama. For example, if the distance between San Francisco and Los Angeles is four hundred miles, then one billionth of that distance is less than one thirty-second of an inch. But physical analogies are not particularly relevant to biological sensitivity. Much less than one part per billion of hormones in human blood can cause profound changes. Similarly, one part per billion of a pollutant in water can do a lot of harm.

Epidemiologists, toxicologists and pathologists often talk about increased health risks from single sources, but they seldom talk (at least publicly) about *overall* environmental risk. Overall environmental risk is the effect on our health of all of the things we come into contact with each day. With regard to water quality, while there have been many studies of individual pollutants, there have been very, very few studies of the combined, or synergistic, effect of pollutants. If, for example, your tap water contains toxic THMs, fluoride, pesticide residue and a substantial level of asbestos, how do these pollutants, in combination, affect your long-term health? Do their harmful effects multiply when they are all present in water at the same time?

Scientists refer to a "safety threshold." This means that if a pollutant in water is below a certain level (say 1 part per million), there is no harmful effect. Of course, nobody knows whether or not this is really true. But assuming it is, what if there are several dozen pollutants in your drinking water (which there probably are) and each of them is present at one part per million—is the water still safe?

What is a "safe" level of pollution, and who is "safe"? With regard to the toxic THMs that are in *every* water supply, the U.S. Environmental Protection Agency currently says a level of 100 parts per million is safe. But the Environmental Council of the European Economic Community (EEC) says that just one part per million is safe.

No one knows what is a safe level of water pollution for any individual—not government health officials, not scientists, not doctors. No one. What we are left with is a giant guessing game whose stakes are human lives. Fortunately, we can rely on common sense, and what common sense suggests is: *You can reduce your overall health risk by reducing your overall toxic load.* In other words, reduce the number of pollutants of all kinds that are in your environment. Water quality is an important factor in that overall equation. Rather than accept so-called "safe" levels of pollution, you should try to reduce *any* pollutants in your drinking water to the lowest possible level.

Finding Out What's In Your Water

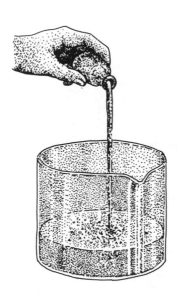

CHAPTER 3

What's Likely To Be In Your Water?

How do you go about finding out what's in your water? Some pollutants are more common in certain areas or types of water systems, while others contaminate water throughout the country. Before you can improve your tap water, you need to know what's in it. This chapter describes what kinds of pollutants to look for in different areas and different types of water systems, and tells you how to find out more exactly, from your water company or through private testing, what is in your water.

Government Water Quality Standards

The Environmental Protection Agency is authorized by the Safe Drinking Water Act of 1974 to set quality standards for drinking water. The states voluntarily follow these standards. In this chapter, one of the things we look at is whether or not your tap water is in compliance with these standards. If you'd like to know exactly what these water quality standards consist of, there is a complete listing of them in Appendix C.

What's Likely To Be In Your Water In A City

City tap water is normally of a higher quality than tap water in a small town or from a private water system. This is because city water is provided by a water utility company whose customer base is large enough that it can afford sophisticated water treatment plants. Although the water delivered by large urban water companies occasionally violates government standards, it is usually within these limits. Unfortunately, if your tap water ever does contain high levels of pollutants, your water company may elect *not* to inform you. One way to find out for sure is to request a copy of your water company's annual water quality report. This should be available without charge, and it will give you the year-long average values for any pollutants in the water, plus the highest level of pollutants detected at any given time during that year.

Your next step is to find out (from your water company) where your water comes from. Is it mostly from ground water or mostly from surface water? If it is from ground water, be on the alert for high levels of radon and toxic metals. If the wells your water company uses are near any industrial facilities, gas stations or landfills, be especially on the alert for toxic organic chemicals in the water. The water company's annual water quality report should detail any presence of these types of pollutants. On the positive side, ground water usually contains high amounts of beneficial minerals (more about this in Chapter 4).

If your water company's source is surface water (which includes lakes, rivers, reservoirs and ponds), be on the alert for the presence of harmful microorganisms, nitrates and organic chemicals. (Note: Water companies are legally required to test frequently for the presence of bacteria but not for parasites. Be sure to ask your water company if it has tested for parasites; also ask your city or county health department if there have been any outbreaks of waterborne diseases, such as giardiasis.)

Try to find out if your water company adds "polyelectrolyte" flocculents to the water. If so, make a note of it. These additives frequently contain cancer-causing chemicals. From your inquiries, make a list of any pollutants that have been detected, regardless at how low a level they were detected (if they were detected at all, chances are they will be present again, sometimes at high levels). Keep your list as a guide in deciding what to do about your water.

What's Likely To Be In Your Water In A Small Town

Public water systems in small towns and rural areas generally do not have the sophisticated treatment plants that cities have. Also, small water systems have less frequent and less stringent testing requirements. In general, small town water systems are more often in violation of government standards than are large, urban systems, and there is a greater chance of high levels of pollutants in a small town water system.

As a first step, ask your local water company for its annul report of water quality. If this is not available, ask to see test results of the treated water for several different dates (for different seasons of the year—some pollutants are seasonal). These tests should clearly show if any pollutants exceed government standards and, if so, by how much.

The source of water determines, to a large degree, what is likely to be in it. If your water supply comes from ground water, it typically contains high levels of minerals, possibly including toxic minerals. As with all ground water, the presence of radon in high concentrations is also a possibility unless the water is aerated as part of treatment before being delivered to customers. If

Surface water is typically low in minerals but is prone to pollution by microorganisms, toxic organic chemicals and nitrates.

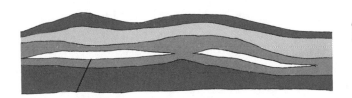

Ground water is typically high in minerals and low in microorganisms. It may contain radon, nitrates, and other organic chemicals.

you live in an agricultural area, be alert for the presence of nitrates, pesticides, herbicides and other organic chemicals. On the positive side, ground water is generally free of harmful microorganisms.

Water from a surface source generally has a low mineral content but is more prone to contamination from runoff and illegal dumping. If your water is from a surface source, inquire about any history of parasites in the water or outbreaks of waterborne diseases. Be on the alert for the presence of organic chemicals in the water. As with ground water, surface water in an agricultural area is highly likely to be polluted with toxic chemicals such as nitrates, pesticides, herbicides and fungicides. Also remember that chlorine combines with organic chemicals to form toxic THMs. And because surface water in an agricultural area is likely to have a high content of organic chemicals, the probability is high that toxic THMs are present in high quantities.

What's Likely To Be In
Your Water In A Private System

In general, the descriptions of ground water and surface water for city and small town public water systems apply to private systems. But private systems, unless carefully designed and maintained, are likely to have the highest levels of pollutants.

If your water comes from a well, you should know whether or not your system is sealed—that is, whether or not the water is exposed to outside air at any point from the well to your faucet. An unsealed well is susceptible to pollution from surface microorganisms. Since well water is high in mineral content, there is a chance that it may contain toxic minerals as well as beneficial ones. Another risk from a well is the presence of radon in the water.

Many private water systems in rural areas are owner-designed and constructed, and they do not have to meet health codes. Typical problem areas for pollution are unsealed well heads, unsanitary springs, or unsealed or open holding tanks. The greatest health risk from these systems is the presence of algae, decaying plant matter, insects and animal waste products, all of which lead to high levels of potentially harmful microorganisms.

Often, water from unsanitary systems looks and smells okay, and families have been drinking this kind of polluted water without apparent harm. But high levels of bacterial and other biological pollution put stress on the human body and make it more susceptible to a variety of diseases seemingly unconnected to the water.

Since you cannot ask for reports from a water utility if you have a private water system, you will need to have the water tested yourself. You should have it tested annually for bacterial pollution, and you should also get a comprehensive lab test at least once a year. Since some pollutants are seasonal, you should stagger the times of the comprehensive tests so that water samples are taken at different times of the year. (Water testing is discussed in more detail later in this chapter.)

Pollutants From The Delivery System If water treatment plants were totally effective in removing all pollutants from water, the water that reaches your house would probably still be polluted. That is because the distribution pipes themselves pollute the water. For example, a large percentage of water in the United States is distributed via cement-asbestos pipes. Microscopic asbestos fibers, which are known carcinogens, enter the treated water from these pipes.

Another type of commonly used distribution pipe is polybutylene, or PB pipe. (PB plastic pipe is easily identified by its distinctive gray color.) PB pipe is porous to toxic solvents such as gasoline and paint thinner, and to many common pesticides and herbicides. Since PB pipe is often used to connect residences to water mains, chemicals used outdoors for gardening and maintenance can pass through the walls of the pipe and enter the water supply coming into a house.

Lead, cadmium and other toxic metals leach out of valves and couplings of pipes between a water treatment plant and a faucet in the home. So even when a water utility carefully monitors its water and is in compliance with government standards, there is a strong probability that the water that comes out of your faucet will have picked up additional pollutants along the way.

What's Likely To Be In Water In The Wild

Crystal-clear, rushing streams; plunging waterfalls; bubbling brooks—all convey an image of freshness and purity. But when you drink from them, you are not the only drinker. Insects drink, too, and some of them lay their millions of eggs in the water. And animals drink, and often leave behind their wastes. One swallow of that fresh-looking (and tasting) water contains literally billions of microorganisms, some harmful and some harmless to humans. Even ice-cold, swiftly-flowing water contains bacteria, viruses and, quite possibly, parasites and worms. The chance of getting sick (sometimes seriously) just isn't worth it, unless it's an emergency and you have no other source of liquid.

There are several compact water filters designed for use in the wild, and I strongly recommend that you use one if you don't have your own water supply with you (these products are described in Chapter 12). Alternatively, boil the water for ten minutes before you drink it.

What's Likely To Be In The Water Of Your Region

It's not possible to generalize about water quality in a geographical region because water sources vary from community to community. For example, residents of New York City and San Francisco receive very high quality water from mountain reservoirs, while many of the communities near these cities use local wells which have been polluted by industrial discharges. Sometimes a water source is far distant from the community it serves. In the case of San Francisco, its water source is in the Sierra Nevada mountains near Yosemite National Park, some 150 miles away.

Ground water sometimes moves great distances through rock strata, so that pollutants from a source many miles away can end up in your water. So even though there are no apparent sources of pollution near the location of your water supply, that is not a guarantee that your water is free of pollutants.

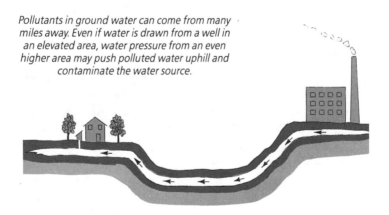

Pollutants in ground water can come from many miles away. Even if water is drawn from a well in an elevated area, water pressure from an even higher area may push polluted water uphill and contaminate the water source.

With private water systems, water quality varies greatly from house to house. For example, in locations where the Environmental Protection Agency has tested wells for the presence of radon, it has been found that one house can have extremely high levels and the adjacent house none.

So if you hear that water in the middle of Wyoming, for example, is very pure, don't assume that *your* water is pure just because you live in the middle of Wyoming.

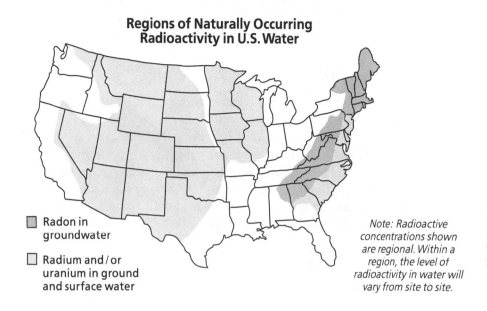

Regions of Naturally Occurring Radioactivity in U.S. Water

◼ Radon in groundwater

☐ Radium and / or uranium in ground and surface water

Note: Radioactive concentrations shown are regional. Within a region, the level of radioactivity in water will vary from site to site.

The light gray areas in the map of naturally occurring radioactivity in U.S. water show parts of the United States where there are generally high levels of radioactivity in water. If you live within one of these areas it doesn't necessarily mean your tap water has dangerous levels of radioactivity, but you should be aware of the possibility. Radon mapping of the United States is still incomplete, but in general the ground formations in the dark gray area extending from Alabama up to Maine are known to have high concentrations of radon. If you live within this area, you should be aware of the *possibility* that high concentrations of radon may be in your water or in the air inside your house.

Pollutants From Within Your Own Home

Even if water could be delivered to your home completely free of all pollutants, it would probably not still be pure when it came out of your faucet. This is because household pipes and plumbing fixtures almost always add some pollutants to the water. The most notorious household source of water pollution is your faucets. They are typically made of a brass alloy that contains some lead. When water remains in contact with the inner walls of a faucet for several hours—overnight, for example—some lead leaches out of the metal of the faucet into the water. If the faucet is not used for wash water the next morning, whoever drinks the first glass of water is likely to get a dose of toxic lead.

Should You Test Your Tap Water?

As I have mentioned, you should not be drinking water straight from the tap no matter where you live or what kind of water system supplies your water. Your options, covered in detail in Chapters 6 through 11, are to drink bottled water or to install a water purifier. So what is the point in spending money to have your water tested if you're not going to be drinking tap water? There are some circumstances in which you should test your tap water even if you're not going to be drinking it.

- *If your water comes from an underground source and the water is not aerated,* whether the source is your own private system or a water utility company, it is important to find out if there is a dangerous concentration of radon in the water. If there is, that radon will be a health threat (from inhalation) wherever water is used in your house. You do *not* need to test for radon if your tap water comes either from a surface source or from an underground source that is aerated during treatment.
- Certain types of toxic organic chemicals are absorbed through your skin when you contact water, as in a shower or bath. Further, hot water allows these chemicals to evaporate rapidly and, like radon, they are harmful if inhaled. These kinds of chemicals are called *volatile organic chemicals* (VOCs), and they can be in any tap water, regardless of where you live or what your source of water is. If your tap water should contain significant levels of these kinds of chemicals, they will be a health threat from water/skin contact even if you improve your drinking water.

Earlier in this chapter I advised you to get a copy of your water company's annual water quality report. While that report will be helpful in many ways, it probably won't identify pollutants such as VOCs. You will need to seek out a technically knowledgeable person who works for the water company and find out if any VOCs have been detected in the water. If none have been detected by the water company, you do not have to test your own tap water for them. If some have been detected, then you should test your own tap water for VOCs—they may have dissipated between the water treatment plant and your faucet—or they may still be in your water.

- If you decide to install a water purifier in your home, and if the annual water quality report from your water company shows substantial levels of pollutants, you should get a comprehensive test of your tap water (as described in Appendix D). The test results will help in determining which kind of purifier you need.

Bogus Vs. Genuine Water Tests

Many of the water tests performed in the United States are deliberately intended to mislead you. That's a strong statement—here's why it's true. A large percentage of water tests are not done by test laboratories but by water purifier dealers. Most of these dealers do not have the sophisticated equipment and expertise that are required to detect a variety of pollutants. What they do have are inexpensive test kits that have been designed to produce dramatic visual effects. The most common of these is the mineral precipitation test. All tap water contains minerals in solution— that is, minerals that are liquefied and transparent; they can't be seen. When something causes them to come out of solution (in water chemistry terms, to *precipitate*), they become visible particles, usually white- or brown-colored.

What the purifier salesman does is to add a chemical to your tap water that causes the minerals to come out of solution, and— presto! There is a heap of strange-looking stuff in the bottom of the glass. This is supposed to demonstrate that your tap water is full of harmful substances and that you need an expensive water purifier or water softener to get rid of them. But the substances are really harmless and are even beneficial minerals, such as calcium and magnesium. Everyone in the industry knows about these "tests" and many legitimate dealers condemn them; but they are still being used on a large scale to deceive customers.

Water purifier dealers sometimes have the capability to perform some additional tests for a few toxic minerals, such as nitrates. But their employees frequently are not adequately trained, not sufficiently careful, or do not have the equipment necessary to get accurate test results. Although dealers sometimes offer their tests free of charge, I strongly advise you not to depend on dealers for testing your water.

What You Need To Know
About Water-Testing Laboratories

Is it possible to know for sure what's in your water without having it tested? No. Is it possible to know for sure what's in your water if you do have it tested? Also no. What testing *can* do for you is to tell you whether or not the major known pollutants are in your water.

There are simply too many possible pollutants to test for all of them. For example, viruses are believed responsible for many waterborn diseases. But there are hundreds of types of viruses, and testing methods do not even exist for half of them. Nevertheless, you can get a lot of useful information from having your water tested.

If you need to have your water tested, be careful in choosing a test lab. It's like choosing a doctor, plumber or auto mechanic—some are better than others. Before you order tests from any lab, ask if it is state-certified for the tests you need and ask what degree of experience the lab has had with those specific tests.

When you receive test results from a water-testing lab, you will see the results for a given pollutant written like this: <0.1 mg/l. This means "less than 0.1 milligram of pollutant per liter of water." What is important to understand here is that the figure of 0.1 mg/l is the smallest amount of the pollutant that that lab can detect, and they didn't find any at that level. So this result doesn't mean that there is zero pollutant in your water, it means that the lab didn't detect any at the sensitivity level of their equipment. The clue to this is to watch for the "less than" sign ($<$). Whenever you see it in a water report, it means that nothing was detected at the most sensitive measuring capability of the lab.

The maximum amounts of pollutants in water that are allowed by government standards are not established for health reasons alone—other practical considerations are involved. For example, the current maximum allowed for a very dangerous and common pollutant—lead—is 50 parts per billion (this seems like a minuscule amount, but lead is highly toxic even in very small quantities). If the lead limit was much lower, many water utilities would be out of compliance and forced to take expensive measures to remove lead down to the lower, more stringent limit.

When water-testing laboratories give you a report on your water, they will point out any pollutants in your water that exceed government standards. That is helpful, except that if pollutants are present, they may be harmful even at levels below the allowable limits. Using the example of lead, let's say your test report comes back showing a level of "30 µg/l" (which means billionths of a gram per liter of water). This is well below the established 50 µg/l limit. But you will have a very dangerous pollutant—lead—in your water. And you need to do something about it.

The Best Water Test Bargains

Testing your water can cost you a lot of money. Here are some typical laboratory charges:

Type of Pollutant	Range of Charges
◆ Common bacteria	$15 – 45
◆ Viruses, each	50 – 300
◆ Parasites, each	35 – 175
◆ Asbestos	35 – 125
◆ Toxic minerals, each	15 – 40
◆ Organic chemicals, each group	60 – 500
◆ Radioactivity from minerals	30 – 200
◆ Radon	60 – 250

If you wanted to test for most of the possible pollutants in your water, here's the approximate cost from a *conventional* lab:

◆ Common bacteria	$ 30
◆ 3 types of viruses at $150 each	450
◆ 3 types of parasites, at $100 each	300
◆ Asbestos	80
◆ 11 toxic minerals, at $25 each	275
◆ 40 organic chemical groups, at $200 each	8,000
◆ 5 radioactivity types, at $60 each	300
◆ Radon	150
Total cost, first round	$9,585

But if your tests found the presence of some pollutants, you would need to test for those again to make sure the first test was not in error. Let's say the lab found a couple of toxic minerals in your water, traces of several organic chemicals, and a fairly high level of asbestos. The cost for retesting would be around $1,000. That brings the total to $10,585. But wait—your water source is surface water, and it is in an agricultural area. Your first round of testing was done in winter, when the land was dormant and not many chemicals were being applied to crops. The runoff of chemicals is expected to be much higher in the spring and summer. So you will need to test your water again.

All told, getting a good picture of what is consistently in your water from a conventional laboratory would cost you somewhere around $20,000!

As you may have guessed by now, most water-testing laboratories are not efficiently set up for consumers. Most of their work is done for cities and counties, water utilites and commercial customers. When you have a test done by one of these labs, it is like buying a pair of handmade shoes—good quality but extravagantly expensive.

Fortunately, there are alternatives—not many, but they exist. In recent years, to meet the needs of consumers for a broad range of water tests, several labs have installed sophisticated, automated testing procedures. They offer comprehensive tests for very low prices. When you order a test from them, you receive a special mailing package. You place your water sample in the mailer, send it to the lab, and receive your report in a couple of weeks. With automated labs such as these, you will need to pay from around $90, for a fairly comprehensive test series, up to around $300 for a complete battery of tests. Here are three of the most popular automated labs with experience and good reputations. Appendix D lists the specific pollutants that these labs test for, and the prices they charge as of this writing.

Spectrum Labs, Inc.
301 West County Road
New Brighton, MN 55112
(612) 633-0101

Home Test
33 South Commercial Street
Manchester, NH 03108
(800) 253-3506

National Testing Laboratories, Inc.
6151 Wilson Mills Road
Cleveland, OH 44143
(800) 458-3330

Tests You Can Do Yourself

Sometimes there is evidence that a particular pollutant is or has been in your tap water and you want to know if it continues to be there. Sometimes you will want to test for it several times over a year to allow for seasonal fluctuations. If the pollutant in question is a common toxic metal, you can buy inexpensive test kits that cost you as little as 50 cents per test and require no previous training to do. These kits usually include enough supplies for dozens of repeat tests. Self-testing kits for common bacteria are also available, but you cannot self-test for organic chemicals. Here are some of the companies that sell these test kits:

Hach Company
P.O. Box 608
Loveland, CO 80539
(800) 227-4224

Environmental Test Systems
P.O. Box 4659
Elkhart, IN 46514
(800) 548-4381

LaMotte Chemical Products
P.O. Box 329
Chestertown, MD 21620
(800) 344-3100

CHEMetrics, Inc.
Route 28
Calverton, VA 22016
(800) 356-3072

While these companies offer a wide variety of mail-order test kits, a few manufacturers have recently begun selling inexpensive, simple water test kits on the retail market. These kits allow you to self-test for a few toxic minerals, but they are for one time only; if you want to retest, you have to buy another test kit. Their advantage is that they are very simple, and anyone can use them. These one-time test kits are sold in hardware and building supply stores.

A Summary Of Actions To Take

- Use the information in this chapter to determine what is most likely to be in your particular tap water. Keep a record of this.

- If your tap water comes from a public water system, get the annual water quality report from your water company and note all pollutants detected. Keep it on file.

- Find out if your water company has tested for the presence of radon in the water. If not, call your regional office of the Environmental Protection Agency and ask them if any radon has been detected in your area.

- If your tap water is from a private water system, you should already be testing it annually for bacteria. In addition, get a comprehensive lab test of it at least once a year, and stagger the times so that the water samples are taken at different times of the year.

- Find out who is the science editor of your local newspaper and ask if there have been any reports of water pollutants in your area.

- If there is any suspicion of pollution other than the normal residual amounts of additives (chlorine, fluoride, flocculents), get a comprehensive test of your water.

- Use all of the information available to you to compile a profile of your tap water. Use the Tap Water Profile worksheet included here to log the information you have gathered. If you are going to be acquiring a water purifier for home use, this profile will help you to decide which kind to get.

Tap Water Profile

	Type of Pollutant	*Name of Pollutant(s)*
Microorganisms	Bacteria	
	Viruses	
	Cysts and other parasites	
Minerals	Toxic metals	
	Nitrates and other non-metals	
	Asbestos fibers	
Organics	Volatiles (VOC's)	
	Pesticides, PCB's, THMs, herbicides, and other non-volatiles	
Radioactives	Radon	
	Uranium and radium, dissolved	
	Uranium and radium, particles	
Additives	Chlorine	
	Fluoride	
	Flocculents, alkalizers, and other water treatment chemicals	
	Organic additives	
Tastes and Smells	Hydrogen sulfide and other volatiles	
	Dissolved minerals	
	Mineral and organic particles	

CHAPTER 4

The Best Drinking Water
For Good Health

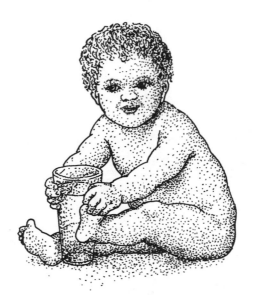

CHAPTER 4

Chapters 2 and 3 described the different types of toxic pollutants that can contaminate your water—pollutants that are health hazards. From all of this information, it might seem reasonable to conclude that the purest water—water that is nothing but water—is the best drinking water. But not all the substances in water are necessarily harmful to your health. In fact, some substances in water are health*giving*.

Drinking Distilled Water

Distilled water is water that has had essentially all of the dissolved substances within it removed—by evaporating it and condensing it back to liquid form. Since about 99 percent of all dissolved matter in water is minerals, distilled water is essentially water that has had all of its minerals removed. The information presented here on distilled water also applies to water that has been demineralized by other methods and is known as *purified*, *demineralized* or *de-ionized* water.

As with fluoridation, there are lots of pro and con arguments about distilled water. The argument in *favor* of drinking it says that the minerals present in water clog up your bodily functions. This theory is partly based on the notion that since calcium (the primary mineral in water) helps to form bones and to harden things in general, it must harden other things in your body as well. Literally dozens of books written by well-meaning doctors, nutritionists and practitioners of holistic medicine claim that essentially all disease is caused by minerals in water—so that by drinking distilled water you will be reinvigorated, your arthritis or hardened arteries will disappear, and so on. These well-meaning authors actually know very little about water chemistry, and the "evidence" they present is heavily biased and without credibility.

An argument *against* drinking distilled water is that you lose a primary source of necessary minerals in your diet, and further, that because the water has lost its own minerals, it attracts and grabs minerals within your body, causing a mineral deficit. This argument has some plausibility. Though we get most of our minerals from fruits and vegetables, and mineral shortages in our bodies are unlikely if a normal diet of mixed foods is eaten, water that has a high mineral content definitely contributes to good health (more on this later in the chapter).

Many people don't like the taste of distilled water, which is often described as tasting "flat." Water bottling companies know that demineralized water doesn't taste as good, and that's why they add minerals to their bottled water after it has been demineralized during the purification process (see Chapter 6 for more information on this).

Care must be taken in the way distilled water is stored, because of its "aggressiveness." Water in its natural state always contains minerals. Demineralized water is in an unnatural condition, and it tries to correct this by combining with any other substances it can. Any substances available to combine with distilled water can only come from the things the water contacts—containers and air, if the containers are open. Since containers are usually closed, and since air is *relatively* free of harmful pollutants, containers are the problem.

No container is completely inert (chemically inactive). Because of its "aggressiveness," distilled water will leach out (combine with) some of whatever the container is made of. Glass is the most inert material for containers, and therefore the safest. Though distilled water is routinely sold in plastic bottles, there is a tendency for the plastic to enter the water over a period of time. (Chapter 6 covers the relative safety of different kinds of water containers.)

I recommend that distilled water, whether purchased in bulk or produced at home by your own distiller, be stored in glass bottles as soon as possible. And if you are drinking distilled water regularly, make sure that your diet contains a good assortment of mineral-rich fruits and vegetables.

Hard Vs. Soft Water

"Hard" water is water that contains large amounts of dissolved calcium and, to a lesser extent, magnesium. "Soft" water is water that contains small amounts of calcium and magnesium. Some water is naturally hard and some is naturally soft. The disadvantage of hard water is that more soap or detergent is needed to get clothing, dishes or other items clean. Also, soft water makes skin feel smoother and hair feel softer. Soft water has one more advantage—it causes less scale. Scale is the hard, whitish stuff that forms on the insides of pipes and tends to clog up the innards of water appliances.

A huge industry exists in the United States whose sole purpose is to make hard water soft, for more efficient washing, smoother skin and softer hair. The desirability of soft water is reinforced by hundreds of water softener manufacturers and thousands of water softener dealers.

Some soft water is naturally occurring, but most soft water consumed in this country is created by water softeners. Water softeners are simple gadgets. What they do is trap calcium and magnesium in the water and replace it with salt (sodium chloride). So when you drink softened water, you're simply drinking water with most of its minerals removed and salt added.

Hard water = high levels of calcium and magnesium

Soft water = low levels of calcium and magnesium

The higher the levels of calcium and magnesium in tap water, the more salt is exchanged. If your incoming tap water has a low level of minerals, your softened water will be low in salt. If your tap water has a high level of minerals, your softened water will have a high level of salt.

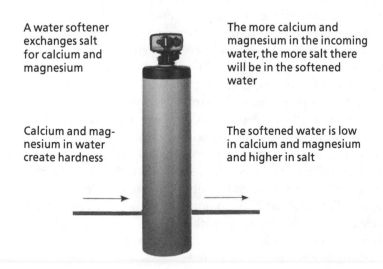

A water softener exchanges salt for calcium and magnesium

The more calcium and magnesium in the incoming water, the more salt there will be in the softened water

Calcium and magnesium in water create hardness

The softened water is low in calcium and magnesium and higher in salt

There has been much publicity, over the years, about the negative health effects of drinking softened water. This sprang from some early research that showed a correlation between cardiovascular disease and high-salt diets. But more recent research has shown that the amount of salt consumed by drinking softened water is insignificant when compared to overall daily salt intake. The only health risk from the added salt in softened water is for persons who are on a severely salt-restricted diet.

WATER SOFTENING TIP

> **Potassium is a health-promoting mineral. If you are using a water softener, potassium can be substituted for salt in your softener. Ask your local water conditioning dealer for "K-Life." If your local dealer can't supply it, call Vigoro Industries, (800) 343-9048, for dealer information.**

The Beneficial Effects Of Minerals In Water

Although we get the majority of the minerals in our diet from fruits and vegetables, the minerals in water play a role in the maintenance of good health. Over the past twenty-five years, research has continued to amass in support of the beneficial role of minerals in water. Studies of populations in areas of naturally occurring hard water (high mineral content) and soft water (low mineral content), have found significantly fewer occurrences of cardiovascular diseases, cancer, diabetes, respiratory diseases, and other health problems in hard water areas.

Almost all of the minerals in water are dissolved. That is, they have liquefied and merged with the water. The standard measure of dissolved minerals in water is called TDS, which stands for total dissolved solids. Studies show that disease is generally less prevalent in areas that have moderate to high levels of TDS in water. High levels of TDS do not seem to provide any advantage over moderate levels; areas with high and moderate TDS levels show the same health improvements when compared to areas

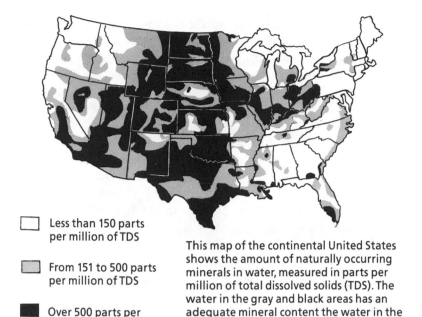

Less than 150 parts per million of TDS

From 151 to 500 parts per million of TDS

Over 500 parts per million of TDS

This map of the continental United States shows the amount of naturally occurring minerals in water, measured in parts per million of total dissolved solids (TDS). The water in the gray and black areas has an adequate mineral content the water in the white areas does not.

with low TDS. What this suggests is that once an adequate minimum intake of beneficial water minerals is available, ingesting more of them doesn't help.

Water From Spas

Dating back to the miracle cures at Lourdes, France, in 1858, spas have enjoyed the reputation of producing superior (health promoting) drinking waters. And if high mineral content were the sole criterion for drinking water quality, this reputation would still be deserved. Spa water, which generally has high levels of beneficial minerals, *should* be superior water. Unlike spas in the United States, European spas are closely regulated, and any potential sources of pollution are prevented by law from operating near them. In spite of this, there have been several instances of toxic pollutants discovered in spot checks of European spa water. The likely source of the pollution is the machinery and the chemicals used in the water bottling process. The discovery of pollutants in spa water has occurred enough times to suggest that these are not isolated incidents, but that they are a recurring problem.

Pollutants have also been found in some spa water in the United States, and I believe the problem is serious enough to recommend that you not drink bottled spa water. Further information on bottled water is given in Chapter 6.

Pollutants Vs. Beneficial Minerals

In the process of removing harmful pollutants from water, the beneficial minerals are sometimes removed as well. When pollutants are present, it is more important to remove them than it is to save minerals. Beneficial minerals can be supplied by diet or by mineral supplements. Most important, the beneficial effects of water minerals on health are less significant than the potential harm that can be caused by pollutants.

How Much Water Should You Drink?

Many articles have been written about the detrimental health effects of not drinking enough water. I won't repeat their warnings here, except to say that every aspect of bodily function can be impaired by insufficient consumption of liquids. In general, the more water you drink, the better your body will be able to neutralize and eliminate harmful substances. An interesting aside is that insufficient water consumption causes the body to gain weight. This is because fat cannot be completely metabolized (converted to energy) without adequate water in the body.

Most people do not drink enough liquids. Health authorities recommend the following minimums for daily consumption of liquids (water, tea, coffee, juice, etc.):

Eight Ounce Glasses of Water Needed per Day

Body weight in pounds	100	125	150	175	200	225	250
Glasses—Average physical activity	5	6	8	9	10	11	12
Glasses—Strenuous physical activity	7	8	10	12	13	15	16

A 150-pound person engaging in average physical activity needs 64 ounces of water, or about eight glasses of liquid per day. A 150-pound person doing strenuous labor needs about twelve glasses per day. Your body can make best use of water if you spread your consumption throughout your waking hours, rather than drinking large amounts at one time.

Health-Giving Water: A Summary

- It is more important to remove any harmful pollutants from your water than to save beneficial minerals in it.

- The healthiest water is that which is free of pollutants but which has a high mineral content.

- Hard water has beneficial minerals that are lacking in soft water.

- If you drink distilled water, make sure it is stored in glass containers.

- Don't drink bottled spa water as your regular daily water.

- Drink lots of pollution-free water each day.

CHAPTER 5

How To Improve Tap Water Without Spending Money

CHAPTER 5

Four Simple Ways To Reduce Pollutants

If you have to drink tap water (and there are times when we all have to), here are some tips that will reduce the pollutants that may be in it.

The Thirty-Second Wait

When water sits motionless in pipes overnight, toxic metals have much more of a chance to leach into the water from pipes and plumbing fixtures. The most notorious culprits are faucets, most of which contain lead. Water that has sat in a faucet overnight or longer will be the most heavily polluted. So when you draw water from a tap that has not been used for a while, allow the water to flow for about thirty seconds before using it for drinking or cooking.

Even when the water has not been standing for a long time, the change in water pressure when you suddenly turn on a faucet can cause pollutants to break loose from pipes and fixtures. So when you are drawing tap water for drinking or cooking, try to remember to turn the water on gradually, then wait about ten seconds before filling your container.

Open Air

When water from a public water supply comes out of the tap, it still has chlorine in it from the disinfecting process. Chlorine in water is volatile—that is, it evaporates easily. Just allowing your tap water to stand in an open container (with a wide mouth, such as a cooking pot) for two or three days will remove most of the residual chlorine.

Boiling

Boiling water for ten minutes is an excellent way to disinfect it, and boiling also removes any remaining chlorine and other volatile pollutants that may be in the water. There has been some criticism of boiling tap water because, it is claimed, non-volatile pollutants become more concentrated as the level of water decreases from the boiling. This is not a valid argument. The amount of water evaporated from ten minutes of boiling is quite small, certainly not enough to significantly concentrate any remaining pollutants.

If you are going to boil your drinking water, use a stainless steel, glass or porcelain pot. Don't use aluminum. Trace aluminum in drinking water has been linked to increased rates of disease—Alzheimer's disease in particular.

Stirring

Stirring tap water in an electric blender at low speed (to avoid splashing) for ten minutes will cause volatile contaminants to evaporate, as in boiling. If you use this method, be sure to do it with the blender cover off to allow for evaporation.

———————

All of the above methods will improve tap water, but they can't remove all of the potential pollutants. Tap water treated by these methods shouldn't be used in place of adequately treated water except for short periods of time.

CHAPTER 6

Bottled Water,
Vended Water,
Bulk Water Stores

CHAPTER 6

Bottled Water

Depending on who you talk to, bottled water can be the best thing to happen to Mankind or the most polluted stuff you can drink. In fact, some kinds of bottled water are very good and some are not good at all—the trick is to know how to pick the good kinds.

There are basically five kinds of bottled water: purified water, drinking water, fluoridated water, natural-source water and specialty water.

The source water for the first three types—purified water, drinking water and fluoridated water—is municipal water, the same water that comes out of your tap. As shown in the following illustration, the bottling company will typically filter the water (to remove dirt and most harmful chemicals), demineralize it (to remove any toxic minerals), and aerate it (to remove any odors by

Typical Processing of Bottled Drinking Water, Fluoridated Water, and Purified Water

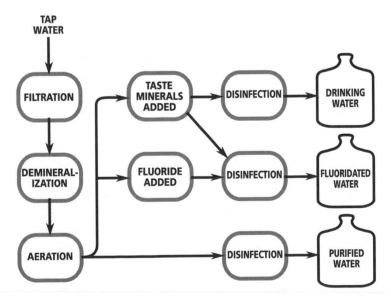

exposing it to air). After having its minerals removed, water tastes "flat," so for the two kinds of water that are sold for drinking— drinking water and fluoridated water—some minerals are re- added to improve taste. For fluoridated water only, fluoride is also added to the water. As the final step before bottling, all three types are disinfected by ozone or ultraviolet light.

Purified Water

Purified water may also be labeled *distilled water, water for distillation uses, de-ionized water,* or *demineralized water.* In addition to having gone through other cleansing processes, each of these labels indicates that the water has had essentially all of its minerals removed and none re-added. So in the sense of there being nothing in it but water, this is the purest water. However, the relevant point is not how "pure" it is, but whether or not it is good for you.

As I explained in Chapter 4, purified water in itself will not harm you, even though minerals in water are definitely beneficial. However, there is a problem specific to bottled purified water. Purified water has had all of its foreign constitutents (which are mostly minerals) removed. This is not a natural state. In the natural state, water contains many different kinds of minerals. Once purified, water will try to return to its natural state by reacting chemically with any material it contacts. Because of this tendency, purified water is "aggressive" water.

When purified water is placed in plastic bottles, it tends to leach out any chemicals in the plastic that are loosely bonded. These chemicals then enter the water (in minuscule amounts). The longer the purified water remains in a plastic bottle, and the higher its temperature, the greater the chance of chemicals entering the water. While there is no overriding evidence to prove that this is harmful, the long-term effect of these chemicals is unknown. Some studies have shown a link between chemicals leached from plastic water bottles and disorders of the human immune system, but this connection is far from conclusive. In my opinion, based upon the research I have surveyed, the "aggressiveness" of purified water may cause long-term health problems. Because of this, I recommend that you do *not* buy purified water in plastic bottles.

Drinking Water

Bottled water that is labeled drinking water is water that has been partially purified, with its minerals allowed to remain, or it is water that has been thoroughly purified (completely demineralized) and then had minerals replaced to improve the taste. Although these minerals are added for taste, they are beneficial for health as well. This brings up a question: are the few kinds of minerals that are re-added to bottled water as beneficial as the wider diversity of naturally occurring minerals that were in the water prior to treatment? No one knows for sure. But what is known for sure is that the added minerals are better than no minerals. Also, adding minerals to drinking water makes it much less aggressive than purified water, so there is less likelihood of toxic chemicals leaching from containers into the water.

Fluoridated Water

The subject of fluoridation in general is covered in Chapter 2. In terms of bottled water, *fluoridated water* is identical to drinking water except that fluoride has been added.

Natural-Source Water

Natural-source bottled water includes all those water products whose source is claimed to be a naturally occurring spring or aquifer (underground reservoir). As I mentioned in Chapter 4, the problem with these products, in general, is that naturally occurring water is not *always* healthy or safe water, even though it generally contains a high level of beneficial minerals. The water from some spas, for example, has been found to contain abnormally high levels of radioactivity; other spring waters have been shown to contain high amounts of toxic organic chemicals and toxic heavy metals, such as lead and cadmium. Even prestige brands of spring water have occasionally been found to contain pollutants. While natural spring water bottlers regularly test their water for several common pollutants, they generally do *not* test for a wide range of possible pollutants. While most natural-source water is safe most of the time, there is no foolproof way to know if a particular brand is safe at any particular time without having it tested.

Specialty Water

Specialty water includes water products with added flavors and/or carbonation, such as lemon-flavored sparkling water. Some of these products use water from naturally occurring springs and some use tap water. Usually sold in small containers, these specialty waters are legally categorized as beverages—that is, it is assumed that, like beer or juice, they will be consumed only occasionally and not daily. Because of this, specialty waters come under a set of regulations that are less stringent than those for drinking water. For occasional use, specialty water products are probably no more or less dangerous than any other bottled beverage.

Recommendations On Bottled Water

- Of the five basic kinds of bottled water (drinking water, purified water, fluoridated water, natural-source water and specialty water), drinking water is the best overall choice.

- Choose a well-known, major brand of drinking water (the large companies generally employ the most effective purification processes and have the best quality control). Appendix E contains a list of bottlers that have been certified by the Food and Drug Administration for sanitary conditions, use of approved materials and containers and quality control.

- Buy bottled water from a store that sells a lot of water (and thus has the water on its shelf for the shortest time).

- Store bottled water in a cool place. Never allow stored water to be in direct sunlight—sunlight increases some microbial growth and allows more chemicals from the container to enter the water.

- Don't drink directly from the bottle—you are transferring millions of microorganisms from your mouth to the water each time you do this.

Vending Machine Water

If you can put up with the inconvenience of lugging your bottles to and from a machine, you should consider vending machine water as a serious alternative to commercially bottled water. When a vending machine is properly maintained, the water it produces is equal to high-quality bottled water.

Vending machine water always uses municipal tap water as its source. And while municipal tap water is not of high quality, it is usually quite consistent. Because of this, and because the purification processes in the machines are well known, the quality of water produced is predictable. In fact, the weak point of vending machine water is not the machine itself but the cleanliness of the containers you use to collect the water.

Each state sets up its own standards for water vending machines. States regulate how the machines must be constructed and what purification methods are used, as well as setting minimum standards for the quality of water produced. County agencies are responsible for enforcing the state standards. Sometimes health inspectors wear two hats—those of both county and state inspectors—at the same time.

The first thing you should look for when you consider using a water vending machine is a seal or label of certification by your state or county. This means, at least in theory, that a particular machine is regularly maintained and inspected. When you find this label on the machine, call your local health department and find out which of the county agencies is responsible for inspecting it and how the agency determines that the machine is being properly serviced. Keep at it until you find out for sure that the machine is being properly maintained. If you run into a dead end with the county, or if you can't find a label of certification on the machine, look for the manufacturer's label (this is legally required to be on it), take down their telephone number and call them. Tell them the location of the machine you want to use and ask them how they service it. If, after all your efforts, you still can't verify that the machine is properly maintained, don't use it.

Typical vending machines have several stages of purification, as shown in the following illustration. In the first stage, a sediment filter traps any dirt or other particles that may be in the water. The second stage of purification is reverse osmosis. This consists of a thin synthetic membrane with ultra-tiny openings, the size of small molecules, which trap chemical pollutants but allow water to pass through. Most pollutants and most, but not all, of the harmless minerals are removed in this process.

Most vending machines allow you to choose between *drinking water* and *purified water* (the latter may also be labeled *distilled* or *de-ionized water*). The only difference between the two is that purified water goes through the demineralization stage and drinking water doesn't. When purified water is selected, the demineralization process removes all remaining minerals from the water. This makes the water suitable for use in steam irons, batteries and other appliances which need purified water.

Typical vending machines have separate storage tanks for drinking water and purified water. When money is deposited in the machine, the type of water selected goes through a carbon filter that removes any remaining traces of chemical pollutants and gives the water a fresh, clean taste. The final stage is disinfection, which kills any microorganisms that may be in the water by means of ultraviolet light.

Typical Vending Machine Purification Process

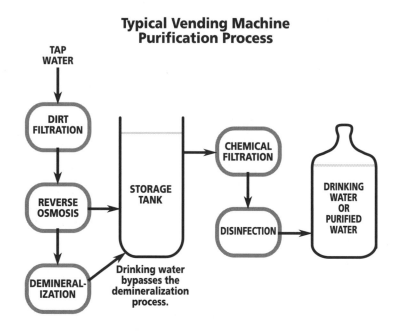

TAP WATER

DIRT FILTRATION

REVERSE OSMOSIS

DEMINERAL-IZATION

STORAGE TANK

Drinking water bypasses the demineralization process.

CHEMICAL FILTRATION

DISINFECTION

DRINKING WATER OR PURIFIED WATER

It is very important that containers you use are free of pollutants. Be sure your containers have not been previously used to store any toxic or unknown substances. Wash your containers thoroughly with detergent and rinse them several times before using. If they are not to be used immediately turn your containers upside-down to let all of the excess water drip out, and let all of the water inside of them dry thoroughly before capping them.

When you fill your bottles with drinking water, cap them and store them away from sunlight and heat. The cooler the storage place, the longer your water will stay fresh. If possible, don't store water for longer than a month (how to store water for emergencies is covered later in this chapter). When water is stored for longer periods it starts to pick up tastes and smells and will eventually grow bacteria and other microorganisms unless it and the containers have been sterilized.

The materials your containers are made of will also affect the quality of your water. All containers, even those made of glass, leach tiny amounts of pollutants into water. In general, glass is best. Next best are bottles made of *rigid,* clear plastic (polycarbonate). Next are containers of stainless steel, which, although they are less prone to pollute than most other metal containers, still do leach tiny amounts of toxic metals into water. Don't use metal containers made of copper or aluminum. If you can avoid it, don't use the soft, cloudy-looking plastic bottles that most bottled water comes in. This kind of plastic has a tendency to migrate— that is, for tiny amounts of it to break free and enter the water, especially when it is exposed to sunlight or used for long periods of time.

Avoid using any plastic containers that were made for purposes other than holding food; utility containers made for non-food use may contain vinyl compounds, which are toxic and can leach into the water. Also, don't use containers with surfaces that bacteria can grow on, such as wood, waxed paper milk cartons, etc.

It is best to have extra containers so you can rotate them. After a bottle has been emptied of drinking water, drain out all excess water and allow the bottle to dry for a week or two, upside-down, with the cap off. Drying the bottles thoroughly will kill most microorganisms that may have started to grow in them. If the water in a bottle starts to have a noticeable taste or smell, discard the water and wash the bottle thoroughly. Washing with disinfectants is also helpful if you rinse the bottles thoroughly after washing.

Recommendations On Vending Machine Water

- Water vending machines generally provide high-quality drinking water *if they are properly maintained.* Be sure to look for the label of certification on the machine and do whatever is necessary to make sure the machine is serviced regularly.

+ Read the description of the purification processes the vending machine employs. This should be stated right on the front of the machine. A few states do not require a final stage of ultraviolet disinfection. If you should find a vending machine without this final stage, it's even more important that you make sure the machine is properly serviced.

+ Choose a machine in a popular location that does a lot of business. In general, the more a machine is used, the less chance there is for any standing water to grow microorganisms. An out-of-the-way machine that stands unused for several days at a time should be avoided.

Bulk Water Stores

There are two kinds of retail stores that sell bulk water: health food stores and water specialty stores. Water from health food stores is usually superior to tap water, but their purification equipment is relatively crude and may not be subject to inspection. Because it is easy to get drinking water that is of known, high quality in most locations, I recommend that you do not purchase drinking water from a health food store (unless the water is from a vending machine that meets the criteria described above).

Water specialty stores (that is, stores that sell only water and water products) offer a very high-quality product. Because these stores specialize in water, their managers usually have a considerable knowledge of water purification, and the in-store equipment is quite sophisticated and is closely monitored and maintained. Like bottled water companies and water vending machines, water stores usually offer both drinking water and purified water. As mentioned previously; drinking water is preferable.

Some water stores offer only purified water that has had its minerals removed by the reverse osmosis process or by distillation. If the water has been treated by reverse osmosis, only about 70–90 percent of its minerals have been removed. If the water has been distilled, about 97–99 percent of its minerals have been removed. This is very pure water that will aggressively combine with any loosely bound materials in containers. So, if you want to drink distilled water, use glass containers or be very sure that your nonglass containers are suitable for this purpose.

Storing Water

All water contains some live microorganisms. Typically, the microorganisms in drinking water are harmless to humans and they are antagonistic to each other—that is, they feed on each other and are self-controlling, at least in the short term. Warmth and sunlight allow microorganisms to grow faster. In general, the longer water is allowed to stand, the higher the level of microorganisms in it will be. For daily drinking water purposes, store water for as short a time as possible

Storing water for emergencies is different. One effective way to store water for emergency use is to sterilize the water once it is in its container by adding an appropriate amount of iodine. Iodine comes in liquid and tablet forms, and can be bought in camping supply stores and drugstores. Iodinated water is for emergency use only—it is not recommended for prolonged, daily use because no one knows the long-term effect of drinking iodinated water.

While filling bottles that are to be sterilized, add the appropriate amount of iodine (as specified on the iodine container) and then fill the bottle completely to the top with water so no air remains when the caps are put on. Carefully seal the caps by wrapping tape tightly around them. When the caps are sealed, turn the bottles on their sides for a while so that the iodinated water contacts the insides of the caps and sterilizes them as well.

Another effective and convenient way of disinfecting water is to keep a small disinfecting water filter at home (see Chapter 12). These filters employ iodine, but none of the iodine enters the water—it just contacts the water as it passes through. In order to use filters, you need stored water on hand. If you are bottling water for later use with an iodine filter, I recommend that you fill the bottles to the top with tap water (which contains residual chlorine that will inhibit bacterial growth), disinfect the bottle caps in boiling water for ten minutes, then screw them on and seal them with tape.

Boiling water for emergency storage is not practical. When you boil it, you lose most of the residual chlorine through evaporation, and the water will not remain sterile when it contacts the inside of the bottles (unless you are able to completely sterilize the bottles).

How
Water Purifiers
Work

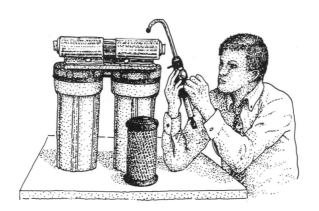

CHAPTER 7

The basic types of water purifiers for home use are

- ◆ **Filters**
- ◆ **Reverse osmosis**
- ◆ **Distillers**
- ◆ **Ultraviolet**

There are other methods of treating water, including aeration, de-ionization, and ozonation, but these are less suited for home use.

How Filters Work

All filters use a substance that traps, absorbs or modifies pollutants in the incoming water. The substance within a filter is called a medium. There are many different kinds of filter media. Some work by mechanically trapping pollutants with an ultrafine sieve action. Others attract pollutants by their electrical charge. And still others employ a process called adsorption, in which pollutants are trapped within the microscopic pores of the medium.

Sediment Filters

Sediment filters work by mechanical sieve action. They are used for removing dirt and other particles from water. If your water comes from a private well, it may contain sand, iron particles and other solids that need to be removed. These kinds of particles are large and require a coarse sediment filter for removal. Water from a public water supply has already had the coarse particles removed, but it still has fine particles remaining. You can't see these fine particles but they can damage the components of a water purifier. To eliminate this problem, a special sediment filter that can trap them is frequently used as the first stage of a drinking water purifier. This protects the other stages from getting clogged.

The following chart shows the relative sizes of common particles. Very small particles are measured in microns (the diameter of a human hair is about 100 microns). Notice that viruses are very small, while sand particles are relatively large. The length of the boxes in the chart shows the smallest to largest size of each type of particle. For example, pollen particles range from about 10 up to 100 microns.

Relative Size of Particles in Microns
(A micron is one-millionth of a meter or 0.0004 inches)

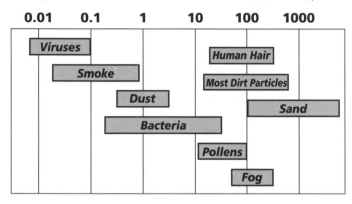

Sediment filters come in many different sieve sizes, from coarse to very fine. They are rated by the smallest particle they will trap. For example, a 5-micron filter will trap all particles that are 5 microns or larger. Sediment filters for use on tap water from public water supplies (which has already been filtered) usually come in three sizes: 5, 10 and 20 microns. A 5-micron filter will provide complete protection for other stages of water purification. A 20-micron filter will provide slightly less protection but will last longer because it won't clog as quickly.

In a private system, if the water is dirty, a coarser filter will be required, typically 50 or 100 microns. This is followed by a finer second-stage sediment filter that protects any additional water purification equipment in use.

Some coarse sediment filters are specifically designed to remove large sand particles. These come in a variety of designs and sizes. But for most home applications, there are three types of sediment filters available: wound string, rigid foam and pleated film. The pleated-film type is generally the most suitable for home use because (1) it has the largest surface area and thus will last longer before it is clogged with dirt buildup, and (2) the thick, wet interior of the wound-string and rigid-foam types tends to support bacterial growth, while the continuous flushing action of the water across the pleated film does not.

Types of Sediment Filters

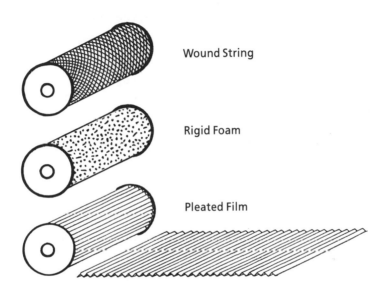

Wound String

Rigid Foam

Pleated Film

Carbon Filters

Carbon filters are used to remove a wide variety of chemical pollutants from water. They are especially effective on organic chemicals such as pesticides, herbicides and industrial chemicals. They are also effective in removing radon, chlorine, and bad tastes and smells. When good-quality carbon filters are properly used, they will remove 80–99 percent of the organic chemicals, radon, chlorine, and bad tastes and smells in water. They will not remove microorganisms or toxic minerals.

REMOVAL OF POLLUTANTS
BY CARBON FILTERS ALONE

Microorganisms	**- No**
Toxic Minerals	**- No**
Organic Chemicals	**- Yes**
Radioactive Substances	**- Radon only; can't remove radioactive minerals**
Additives	**- Will remove chlorine but not other additives**
Tastes and Smells	**- Yes**

The carbon in water filters is called *activated* carbon. This kind of carbon is made by specially heating wood, coconut or coal so that it forms millions of microscopic pores. These pores attract and trap pollutants in water. There are two forms of carbon in wide use: granular and block. Carbon granules are about the size of coarse sand. Carbon block is finely powdered carbon that has been bound together into a rigid solid.

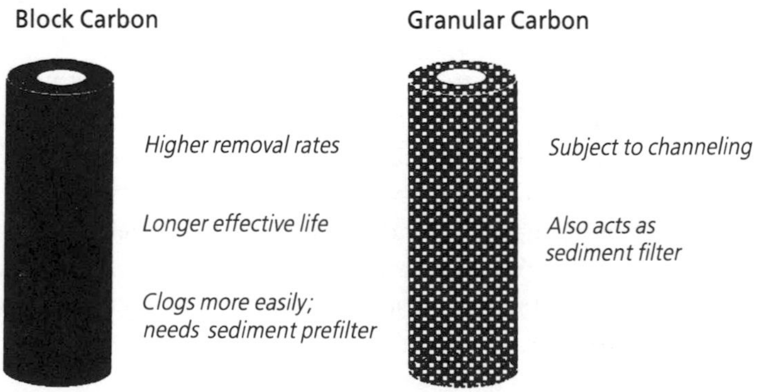

Block Carbon

Granular Carbon

Higher removal rates

Longer effective life

Clogs more easily; needs sediment prefilter

Subject to channeling

Also acts as sediment filter

All other things being equal (such as size), a carbon block filter will remove higher percentages of pollutants and will last longer than a granular carbon filter. Because the granules in granular carbon are free to move, when water passes through a granular carbon filter it will try to find the shortest and easiest path. This creates channels, so that the water flowing through the filter does not contact all of the carbon. Channeling can be minimized by proper design of the filter housing, but it cannot be eliminated completely.

A carbon block filter has the disadvantage of needing a sediment prefilter so that its dense pores are not clogged by dirt or mineral particles. A granular carbon filter, in contrast, acts as its own sediment filter.

Effective carbon filtration depends on several things. The most important are (1) the amount of time the water contacts the carbon (the slower the flow, the more effective the filtration), (2) the density of the carbon (carbon block is more effective than granular carbon, and fine granular carbon is more effective than coarse granular carbon), (3) the quantity of carbon (the larger the filter, the more effective the filtration), and (4) the amount of water that has passed through the carbon (the fresher the carbon the better the filtration).

Like most filters, carbon filters accumulate pollutants within the filtering medium. This creates two potential problems. The first is that, with changes in water pressure, accumulated pollutants can break away and cause some unlucky person to ingest a large dose of pollution. The second drawback is that the inside of a carbon filter provides a supportive environment for the growth of certain kinds of bacteria. While these bacteria have not caused any disease symptoms, no one knows for sure how ingesting them affects human health.

Some manufacturers add a bacterial growth inhibitor to the carbon. This is usually a silver compound. Unfortunately, tests show that in actual use the silver does not do very much to reduce bacterial growth in most filters.

The potential problems of pollutant breakaway and bacterial growth can be minimized by replacing the carbon medium at regular designated intervals and by not using the first flow out of the filter in the morning, after the water has been standing all night. When you first turn on the tap in the morning, you should allow the filtered water to flow for about thirty seconds before using it. This procedure should be repeated whenever the filter is unused for more than a few hours.

A carbon filter medium has a finite lifetime. A household of four people typically uses about 1½ gallons of drinking water per day, or 2½ gallons per day if filtered water is also used for cooking. This translates into approximately 500 to 1000 gallons per year. Many filter manufacturers claim a 2000-gallon or more life for their carbon filters, but I recommend that carbon filters be changed every six months, for optimum performance and to minimize the chances of pollutant breakaway.

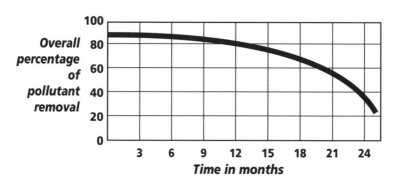

**Carbon Filter Performance
At Time Intervals**

Some manufacturers include a valve in the filter so that water flow through the carbon can be reversed. This is called backwashing. It is supposed to regenerate the carbon so that it will perform as new. While carbon backwashing will remove much of the accumulated sediment within the filter, it generally is *not* effective in removing chemical pollutants from within the pores of the carbon. Because of this and because it increases the potential for pollutant breakaway, I do not recommend backwashing a carbon filter that is used for drinking water.

Sometimes carbon filters are installed in private water systems where the water has not been disinfected. This usually results in a large and potentially harmful buildup of bacteria within the filter. Unless some method of disinfection is also used ahead of the filter, a carbon filter should not be used in a private water system.

If you use a carbon filter, the main things to remember are

- Avoid using the first flow: wait thirty seconds in the morning.

- Use a slow flow rate: one-half gallon per minute or less (the stream of water should be narrower than a pencil).

- Replace the carbon at regular intervals. If the output water begins to smell or taste bad, disard the carbon immediately.

Filters For Microorganisms

Of the three basic classes of waterborne microorganisms—viruses, bacteria and parasites—bacteria and parasites can be removed by specially designed filters, but viruses cannot because they are too small.

In theory, carbon block filters should be able to remove bacteria and parasites from water because the micron rating of these filters—the smallest size of particle they trap—is smaller than most of the bacteria and all of the parasites found in water. But in practice the carbon is not uniform enough to insure that these microorganisms are trapped. Also, the seals within these filters are not 100 percent secure; some leakage occurs around the carbon medium. For these reasons and because of the previously mentioned bacterial growth within the carbon, *no carbon filter, by itself, should be used for microorganism removal.*

In water treatment, there is an important distinction between *removing* bacteria from water and simply *stopping their growth* within the filter. Many filters are labeled *bacteriostatic.* This means that bacteria do not multiply within the filter. It does *not* mean that the filter *removes* all bacteria from water. While many filter manufacturers claim that their product is bacteriostatic, very few filters actually remove all bacteria from water.

There are two types of filters that remove bacteria and parasites from water: the membrane filter and the ceramic filter. Both types come with absolute seals—that is, there is no water leakage around the filter medium. All antibacterial filters need to be periodically cleaned. When bacteria and other microorganisms are trapped on a surface, they eventually build up a film that clogs the filter. Membrane filters can be washed, but they are more delicate and cannot take harsh cleaning. Ceramic filters, on the other

Pleated membrane filter   Porous ceramic filter

hand, are sturdier and can be scrubbed over and over without harm. In general, ceramic filters are more convenient for home use. Their only disadvantage is that they can break if dropped.

Mineral / Metal Filters

While some sediment filters and some carbon filters can remove lead in water that is in the form of particles, these filters cannot remove lead or other toxic metals that are *dissolved* in water. In recent years, several new kinds of filter mediums have been developed to remove dissolved lead and other toxic metals from water. Two of these have proved to be very effective. The first is alumina. This is an aluminum compound that strongly attracts and traps metals that are dissolved in water. While alumina traps toxic metals, it does not remove chlorine, organic chemicals or microorganisms. Like carbon filters, the performance of an alumina filter decreases with use. When used for the specific purpose of removing lead from water, a small alumina filter installed in a kitchen lasts for about 2,000 gallons, or up to two years of average use.

The other recent addition to the types of filters available is the redox filter. The term *redox* is an abbreviation of "reduction-oxidation," which is a chemical exchange process. In a redox filter, toxic metals in the water are exchanged with harmless zinc and copper. The zinc-copper in the filter also traps chlorine and smells caused by hydrogen sulfide, and it greatly reduces (but does not totally eliminate) any bacteria in the water. One of the other advantages of a redox filter is that, unlike other filter mediums, it does *not* accumulate pollutants. Lead, chlorine and other pollutants are converted to harmless zinc and copper compounds. Because of this, the zinc-copper medium within the filter has an extremely long life; recent tests have shown no reduction in its effectiveness after several years of use.

While other forms of water purification, such as distillation and reverse osmosis, can also remove lead and other toxic metals from water, until recently there has been no way to remove these pollutants with the simpler method of filtration. The alumina and redox filters are an important and useful addition to drinking water treatment.

How Reverse Osmosis (RO) Works

Osmosis is the passage of molecules through the microscopic pores of a living or synthetic membrane. In normal osmosis, if there is a difference in concentration of molecules between one side of the membrane and the other, the more concentrated molecules will pass through the membrane to equalize the concentration on both sides.

In reverse osmosis water treatment, a thin synthetic membrane is used. Its pores are large enough to pass water molecules but too small to pass larger molecules. Water pressure forces water molecules through the membrane but leaves the larger molecules of pollutants behind. The process is called *reverse* osmosis because instead of equalizing the concentration of substances on either side of the membrane (as in osmosis), the water pressure creates pure water on one side and a concentrate of pollutants on the other. The pure water is channeled to the RO output, and the water containing pollutants (as well as minerals) is channeled to a drain.

RO is a very slow process because water molecules must individually pass through very small pores in the membrane. An RO membrane is tightly coiled within a cylinder to provide a large surface area, but it still takes several hours for enough water to pass through the membrane to produce a gallon of water. Because the RO process is so slow, small storage tanks, holding two to five gallons, are used. When drinking water is drawn from the RO faucet, the water comes from the storage tank. The RO unit then slowly refills the tank.

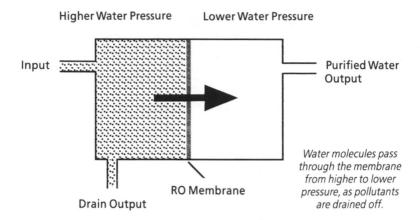

Higher Water Pressure   Lower Water Pressure

Input

Purified Water
Output

*Water molecules pass
through the membrane
from higher to lower
pressure, as pollutants
are drained off.*

RO Membrane

Drain Output

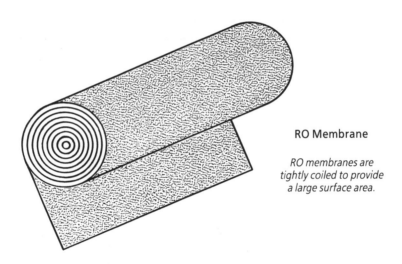

RO Membrane

*RO membranes are
tightly coiled to provide
a large surface area.*

Most RO purifiers waste water. Between three and ten gallons of tap water are needed to produce one gallon of purified water; the remainder is drained away. (The amount of purified water produced in comparison with the total amount of water used is called the *recovery rate*.) However, a few RO designs are more efficient. In a *recirculating* RO, drain water is reused several times, reducing water wastage. And an *in-line* RO uses the normal flow of water through household pipes, so there is no water wastage.

REMOVAL OF POLLUTANTS
BY REVERSE OSMOSIS ALONE

Microorganisms	- Partial
Toxic Minerals	- Yes
Organic Chemicals	- Yes
Radioactive Substances	- Can't remove radon; can remove most radioactive minerals
Additives	- Can't remove chlorine
Tastes and Smells	- No

An advantage of RO units over filters is that they remove a wider variety of pollutants. A good quality RO unit will remove 80–98 percent of most toxic minerals and organic chemicals from water. ROs cannot, however, remove radon or chlorine. In theory, microorganisms, which are much larger than the molecule-size pores of an RO membrane, should all be rejected by the membrane. But in practice the pores of the membrane are not uniform enough to insure the removal of *all* microorganisms. Because of this, RO units, by themselves, cannot be used for disinfecting water.

There are several installation restrictions on RO units. They cannot be installed on a private system unless the water has been disinfected. High levels of dissolved minerals in water (TDS, or total dissolved solids) adversely affect the membranes. The performance of RO units is also proportionate to water pressure: the higher the pressure, the better the performance. RO units installed in a low-pressure system (water pressure below 40 pounds per square inch [psi]) require a special booster pump to increase the pressure. Where tap water comes from a public water system, and the water quality is known, there is usually no difficulty in operating an RO unit. But on private water systems, several water tests must be done before determining whether or not an RO can be used.

Unlike filters, RO membranes do not accumulate any pollutants—the pollutants are constantly being washed away. And since there is no accumulation of pollutants there is no chance of pollutant breakaway as there is with filters. However, the RO membrane itself degrades with use. With clean, city water, a typical membrane lasts two to three years before it must be replaced. If there are bacteria in the water, if the water has a high TDS (total dissolved solids) level, or if there are other adverse conditions, an RO membrane can fail prematurely, often after just a few months.

Testers are available that can check the performance (and thus the condition) of an RO membrane in a few seconds, simply by pressing a button. These testers are inexpensive and should be installed with every RO unit.

Membranes for RO units are made of two types: cellulose acetate (CA) or of thin film composite (TFC). TFC membranes outperform CA membranes and last longer. They are also slightly more expensive. Their disadvantage is that they cannot tolerate chlorinated water. If your tap water is chlorinated and you want to use an RO with a TFC membrane, you will also need to install a chlorine prefilter.

While RO units provide an efficient means of removing a wide variety of pollutants from water, they are almost never used alone. They invariably come as part of an integrated, combination system in which filters are also employed. Combination systems are discussed in detail in Chapter 8.

How Distillers Work

Distillation is a simple, proven, dependable method of removing pollutants from water. Water is boiled and produces steam. The steam is cooled and condenses back into water. Any substances that cannot evaporate are left behind in the boiling chamber. Distillation removes the widest variety of pollutants from water of any single purification method. But there is one type of pollutant that distillation does not remove well, and that is the class of organic chemicals known as volatile organics (VOCs), which evaporate easily.

REMOVAL OF POLLUTANTS
BY DISTILLATION ALONE

Microorganisms	- Yes
Toxic Minerals	- Yes
Organic Chemicals	- Partial (removes all organics except volatiles)
Radioactive Substances	- Yes
Additives	- Yes
Tastes and Smells	- Yes

Like reverse osmosis, distillation is a very slow process. The average distiller takes five to six hours to make one gallon of distilled water. And like RO units, distillers store water in a tank or bottle for when it is needed. Distillation takes a lot of power. Depending on the distiller selected and the price of electricity, it costs 25 to 35 cents per gallon to make distilled water (cost-per-gallon comparisons are in Chapter 9). There is also the problem of heat generated. If the distiller is located inside the house (as opposed to in the garage, for example), it will help warm the house in winter but will also add to the heat in summer.

One of the fundamental differences between distillation and all other types of water purification is that distillation is very reliable. If the distiller is operating, the quality of the water it produces will be consistent. There is no decrease in performance over time; a ten-year-old distiller will produce the same quality of water as a new one. With a distiller, there is no requirement to replace filters or RO membranes at regular intervals. Also, a distiller is not so dependent on manufacturing quality control as other water purifiers. A filter, for example, may be advertised as performing up to a certain level, but the actual unit you buy may or may not perform that well, depending on the manufacturing standards.

There are two basic types of distillers made for home use: air-cooled batch distillers and water-cooled, continuous flow distillers.

Air-Cooled Batch Distiller

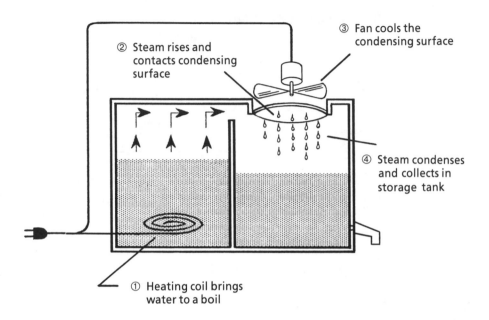

② Steam rises and contacts condensing surface

③ Fan cools the condensing surface

④ Steam condenses and collects in storage tank

① Heating coil brings water to a boil

Air-cooled distillers are all batch distillers. This means that the boiling chamber is filled with tap water and the distiller operates until all or most of the water is evaporated and collected in a storage tank. The distiller produces one batch at a time.

A heating coil heats the water until steam is produced. The steam is then dircted to a condensing surface that is cooled by a fan. When the steam contacts the cool surface it condenses back into water and drips into the storage tank. Very little water is wasted in this process. A batch distiller typically converts about 95 percent of tap water into distilled water, with 5 percent lost as vapor to the surrounding air.

In a water-cooled distiller, the boiling chamber is always kept full by a constant trickle of incoming tap water. When steam is produced, it is directed to a condensing surface. After contacting the condensing surface the steam reverts to water and drips

Water-Cooled, Continuous Flow Distiller

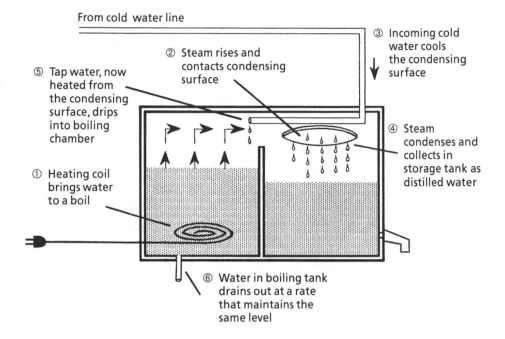

From cold water line

② Steam rises and contacts condensing surface

③ Incoming cold water cools the condensing surface

⑤ Tap water, now heated from the condensing surface, drips into boiling chamber

④ Steam condenses and collects in storage tank as distilled water

① Heating coil brings water to a boil

⑥ Water in boiling tank drains out at a rate that maintains the same level

into the storage tank. The condensing surface is kept cool by the incoming trickle of cold tap water. Through contact with the condensing surface, the cold tap water is heated and drips into the boiling tank. This design is more energy efficient because when water enters the boiling tank it is already hot—not as much energy is required to turn the water to steam, and less heat is wasted by being transferred to the surrounding air.

There is another advantage to the water-cooled distiller. The flow of tap water into the unit is adjustable. If the flow is decreased, less water flows past the condensing surface. This means the incoming tap water will get hotter. If the input flow is increased, more water will flow past the condensing surface and the incoming tap water will remain cooler.

Now remember that distillers are good at removing all pollutants except volatile ones. Volatile pollutants typically evaporate at lower temperatures than boiling water. If air vents are located near the tap water, after it has been heated, volatile pollutants in the tap water will evaporate into the air *before* the tap water reaches the boiling chamber. This means that volatile pollutants never reach the boiling chamber and therefore will not be in the steam that is produced. Further, the temperature of the heated tap water can be adjusted to most effectively remove particular volatile pollutants that are known to be in your tap water.

While water-cooled distillers are more energy-efficient than the air-cooled ones, and can remove more volatile pollutants, water-cooled distillers waste water. They are also a bit more complicated and less foolproof than the air-cooled variety.

How Ultraviolet (UV) Works

Ultraviolet, or UV, is a radiation that is higher in the spectrum than visible light. It is known to be effective in killing bacteria and other microorganisms. The only types of microorganisms that cannot be killed by ultraviolet are those with hard coverings, such as giardia cysts. Ultraviolet purifiers are made for the specific purpose of disinfecting water and are not effective in removing other pollutants.

REMOVAL OF POLLUTANTS
BY ULTRAVIOLET ALONE

Microorganisms	- Yes, except cysts
Toxic Minerals	- No
Organic Chemicals	- No
Radioactive Substances	- No
Additives	- No
Tastes and Smells	- No

Most materials, including common glass, do not transmit ultraviolet radiation efficiently. One of the best transmitters of UV radiation is quartz glass, and it is used for most UV lamps. In order for a UV unit to disinfect water effectively, three conditions must be met: (1) the UV lamp must produce above a critical intensity of radiation; (2) the water must be subject to this radiation for a minimum period of time; and (3) the water must be clean. UV units employ many different designs to meet the first two conditions. The following illustration shows two simple designs: (1) where water flows straight through a cylinder past a long tubular UV lamp and (2) where the water conduit is wound in a spiral to slow the passage of the water past the UV lamp. In the spiral design, the spiral tubing must also be of quartz glass in order to transmit UV energy efficiently.

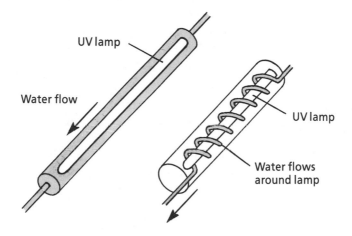

To meet the third condition—clean water—prefilters must *always* be used. If the water should contain particles, bacteria and other microorganisms will be shielded from the UV radiation and will pass through the unit unscathed. Because water cleanliness is so critical to UV operation, all UV units for home use need to be designed for easy cleaning access.

UV adds nothing to water and takes nothing away. The advantage of this is that no toxic disinfectant remains in the water, as with chlorine disinfection. The disadvantage is that, if microorganisms enter the water at any point after the UV treatment, there is no residual disinfectant to kill them.

Alternative Methods

In addition to the primary methods of purifying water at home—filtration, reverse osmosis, distillation and ultraviolet—other methods are sometimes used. One of these is *de-ionization* (DI). DI employs a tank of synthetic materials that attract and trap minerals as water passes through them. Like distillation, DI removes essentially all minerals from water. It does not remove other types of pollutants. DI is used when minerals must be completely removed from water and distillation is impractical.

Another method for removing certain pollutants is *aeration*. Aeration simply means exposing water to lots of air. Aerators are used almost exclusively on private water systems. They have been traditionally used to remove bad smells (especially the rotten-egg odor of hydrogen sulfide) from water. More recently, they are also being used to remove radon and other volatile pollutants.

There are two kinds of aerators: pressurized and atmospheric. *Pressurized* aerators employ air injectors that force air into a water line without losing water pressure. This type of aerator is not suitable for removing radon from water. An *atmospheric* aerator operates quite differently. It employs a nozzle that sprays a fine mist of water into an open tank. This allows volatile pollutants to evaporate into the surrounding air. This type of aerator is very effective at removing volatile pollutants. Its disadvantage is that when water is sprayed into the tank, water pressure is lost, and an additional pump is needed to repressurize the water.

Ozonation is sometimes used to disinfect drinking water in place of chlorine or ultraviolet treatment. Ozone is a toxic form of oxygen (O_3 rather than O_2 of ordinary oxygen). It is a very powerful and effective disinfectant that works by chemically burning up pollutants. However, its technology as a home drinking water treatment is not well developed and it tends to burn up purification equipment as well as pollutants. Also, some of the ozone that is generated escapes from water into the air. So when an ozonator is used indoors, it may raise the ozone concentration to a harmful level.

CHAPTER 8

Improving Performance By Combining Types Of Purifiers

CHAPTER 8

B ecause no single method of water purification can remove all potential pollutants, almost all water purifiers for home use combine more than one method. This is made easier by the availability of standardized, interchangeable cartridges for all types of filters. Because they are easily interchangeable, a water purification system can be designed to work most effectively on your particular tap water. Unfortunately, many water equipment dealers are either unaware of the variety of units available or unwilling to offer them for sale. But the proper combinations are the key to effective drinking water treatment.

Distiller Combinations

Although water purifiers sold for home use almost always combine methods of treatment, distillers can be the exception. Because distillers, by themselves, remove almost all pollutants from water, they are often sold alone. Notice in the illustration of distiller combinations that there is one difference between the two systems. The distiller alone only partially removes organic pollutants—it doesn't remove all volatiles. But with the simple addition of a carbon filter, any distiller can remove *all* types of pollutants.

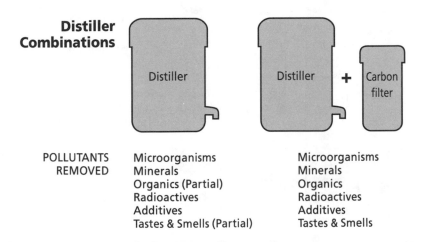

Distiller Combinations

Distiller

Distiller **+** Carbon filter

POLLUTANTS REMOVED

Microorganisms
Minerals
Organics (Partial)
Radioactives
Additives
Tastes & Smells (Partial)

Microorganisms
Minerals
Organics
Radioactives
Additives
Tastes & Smells

Filter Combinations

As described in Chapter 7, several types of filters are available for home use. The most effective of these are sediment, bacterial, redox and carbon filters. Notice the differences in the systems shown in the illustration of filter combinations. The first combination is a carbon filter with a sediment filter ahead of it to protect it from clogging. Together these do a good job of removing many pollutants, but they can't remove such things as bacteria or toxic lead. Adding more filters improves the system's effectiveness. In the system at the bottom, four different types of filters work together to remove almost all pollutants. While this system still can't remove certain kinds of toxic minerals (such as nitrates and radioactive uranium), it is a very effective combination.

POLLUTANTS REMOVED

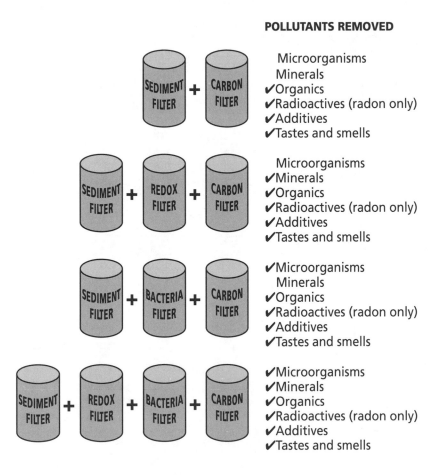

Microorganisms
Minerals
✔Organics
✔Radioactives (radon only)
✔Additives
✔Tastes and smells

Microorganisms
✔Minerals
✔Organics
✔Radioactives (radon only)
✔Additives
✔Tastes and smells

✔Microorganisms
Minerals
✔Organics
✔Radioactives (radon only)
✔Additives
✔Tastes and smells

✔Microorganisms
✔Minerals
✔Organics
✔Radioactives (radon only)
✔Additives
✔Tastes and smells

Reverse Osmosis Combinations

Because of the delicacy of the RO membrane, reverse osmosis purifiers are always sold with a sediment filter to clean the water ahead of it. And because RO membranes do not remove all organic pollutants and tastes and smells from water, these systems also come with a carbon filter. At the top of the reverse osmosis illustration, notice that a basic RO system, with sediment and carbon filters, still does not remove all pollutants. Microorganisms can get through as well as some toxic minerals. Additional filters make the RO system more effective. Notice that the RO system at the bottom of the illustration is capable of removing *all* types of pollutants from water.

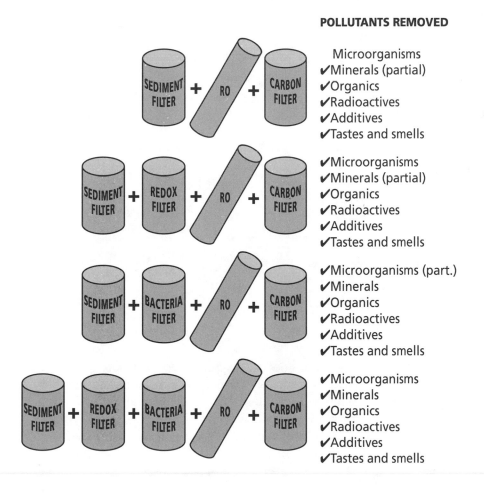

POLLUTANTS REMOVED

Microorganisms
✔Minerals (partial)
✔Organics
✔Radioactives
✔Additives
✔Tastes and smells

✔Microorganisms
✔Minerals (partial)
✔Organics
✔Radioactives
✔Additives
✔Tastes and smells

✔Microorganisms (part.)
✔Minerals
✔Organics
✔Radioactives
✔Additives
✔Tastes and smells

✔Microorganisms
✔Minerals
✔Organics
✔Radioactives
✔Additives
✔Tastes and smells

Ultraviolet Combinations

As explained in Chapter 7, ultraviolet purifiers are never used alone; they must be preceded by a sediment filter in order to be effective. In the illustration of ultraviolet combinations, notice that the top system only removes microorganisms. Even within that category, it cannot kill giardia cysts. The only time UV is used without additional filters is when its only purpose is to disinfect the water by killing bacteria. If a carbon *block* filter is added to the system, it traps the cysts that pass through the UV unit unscathed, and the removal of microorganisms is thorough. When a redox filter is also added, toxic minerals are removed as well, and the system can remove all pollutants except radioactive metals such as uranium and radium.

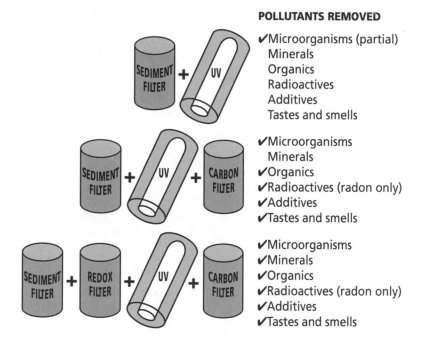

POLLUTANTS REMOVED

✔Microorganisms (partial)
Minerals
Organics
Radioactives
Additives
Tastes and smells

✔Microorganisms
Minerals
✔Organics
✔Radioactives (radon only)
✔Additives
✔Tastes and smells

✔Microorganisms
✔Minerals
✔Organics
✔Radioactives (radon only)
✔Additives
✔Tastes and smells

Most tap water does not require extensive combinations of water purification methods in order to be reasonably safe, but *some* combination of methods *is* generally required. It's also important to know that some types of purifiers, employing a single method of purification, are sold with the claim that they will remove all harmful pollutants from water. This is simply not true.

CHAPTER 9

Evaluating Water Purifiers

CHAPTER 9

Bogus Claims

Up to this time, the water purification industry has been largely unregulated. Some states have recently legislated standards for the performance of purifiers and the claims of manufacturers and sellers, but there is still a lot of bogus advertising going on. One of the purposes of this book is to give you enough accurate information so that you will not be misled by false claims.

Here is a sample of misleading claims from a recent advertisement, which uses a chart to compare the manufacturer's RO unit ("Brand X") with bottled water and carbon filters:

Note: This chart is an example of a misleading claim

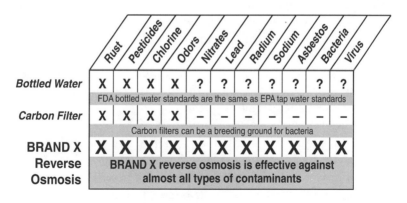

	Rust	Pesticides	Chlorine	Odors	Nitrates	Lead	Radium	Sodium	Asbestos	Bacteria	Virus
Bottled Water	X	X	X	X	?	?	?	?	?	?	?
	FDA bottled water standards are the same as EPA tap water standards										
Carbon Filter	X	X	X	X	–	–	–	–	–	–	–
	Carbon filters can be a breeding ground for bacteria										
BRAND X Reverse Osmosis	X	X	X	X	X	X	X	X	X	X	X
	BRAND X reverse osmosis is effective against almost all types of contaminants										

In promoting its own RO system, this manufacturer has stretched the truth quite a bit. For example, the chart shows that Brand X RO removes bacteria and viruses. This isn't accurate. While ROs do remove *some* microorganisms, they cannot remove them all and manufacturers cannot legally make this claim. ROs are also notoriously poor at removing nitrates from water, yet the chart claims that Brand X can remove them.

The comments within the chart are also misleading. In an attempt to discredit bottled water, the chart states that "FDA bottled water standards are the same as EPA tap water standards."

(The Food and Drug Administration [FDA] and the Environmental Protection Agency [EPA] are both federal agencies.) While it is true that bottled water need only meet tap water standards under current *federal* law, it must also meet the requirements imposed by state laws and, for most bottlers, the standards of the bottled water association as well. In practical terms, the statement about FDA and EPA standards is meaningless.

The chart also states that "Carbon filters can be a breeding ground for bacteria." That is true. What is left unsaid is that the Brand X RO, which itself comes with a carbon filter, can also be a breeding ground for bacteria.

After surveying water purifier advertising for several years, I have come to the conclusion that much of it is incomplete, misleading or just plain false. Often this is deliberate. For example, filter manufacturers often claim that their products remove the toxic lead from water. While this is true of a few filters that are specifically made to remove lead, most general-purpose water filters cannot do it. So how can manufacturers make this claim? They do so through a slim and misleading technicality. There are two forms of lead in water: solid particles of lead and lead that is dissolved in the water. Most filters can only remove the solid particles. The problem is that almost all lead in water is dissolved and not solid. So even though a filter may remove only 1 percent of the harmful lead in the water, the manufacturer may—misleadingly—advertise it as removing lead.

Another advertising trick is the use of the world *bacteriostatic*. It's an impressive word, and it sounds like something that's very bad for bacteria. As I explained earlier, it means that bacteria will not *grow* within the unit. But if there are bacteria in the incoming water, there will also be some bacteria in the water produced by a bacteriostatic purifier—it doesn't *remove* all bacteria. In order to disinfect water thoroughly, a purifier must be a *sterilizer*. Nevertheless, "bacteriostatic" products are wrongly being sold for installation in bacterially contaminated water supplies.

In general, you should not believe *any* performance claims or comparisons that are made by a water purifier manufacturer. Sometimes manufacturers claim that their performance data are backed up by "laboratory tests." While some of these tests are valid, many are not, and you need to be a water expert to be able to tell the valid ones from the invalid ones.

Product Testing Organizations

If you can't trust manufacturers and dealers, whom can you trust? In past years, the Environmental Protection Agency has sponsored testing of water purifiers. Unfortunately, these tests have been incomplete and have only included a small number of products. Some states have moved ahead of the federal government on product testing. In particular, as of this writing, water purifiers sold in California, Iowa and Wisconsin must be objectively tested. Massachusetts and New York also have product certification programs but they are less effective.

Consumer magazines should, in theory, be good sources for accurate information on water purifiers. From time to time, these magazines test purifiers and report the results in their publications. I have monitored the test results in these publications and have found them very useful. At the same time, they have some serious flaws.

For example, in reporting on distillers, the consumer magazines have tested only a few types of distillers and, from those results, have incorrectly generalized about the performance of *all* distillers. In evaluating a group of water filters they may only test the products' performance in removing a single pollutant and use the results of that test to generalize about overall product quality. That can be misleading because the performance of products can vary widely with different pollutants.

There are also two private testing organizations of national scope: the Water Quality Association (WQA) and the National Sanitation Foundation (NSF). For years the WQA has been a major trade association for manufacturers and dealers of water treatment products, particularly water softeners. The WQA now has a product certification program for drinking water purifiers and, while this is a step in the right direction, the organization has a long way to go to overcome its reputation of bias in favor of manufacturers.

Probably the most reputable testing organization for water purifiers is the NSF. Their staff is very knowledgeable and the organization applies rigorous standards in all of their product tests. If you need more information on specific products than this book provides, I recommend the NSF as a source. Their address is

National Sanitation Foundation
P.O. Box 1468
Ann Arbor, MI 48106
(313)769-8010

Comparing Purifier Performance

The water purifiers available for sale vary greatly in their performance. For example, a small carbon filter that snaps onto a kitchen faucet is generally ineffective, while a larger carbon filter can do an impressive job of removing pollutants. Given these differences, if average performance ratings included the worst and best of products, the results would be meaningless—they would tell you very little about either the good products or the bad ones. Because of this, and because the purpose of this book is to guide you toward products that work well, the Water Purifier Performance Chart included here is based *only on top-performing products*.

The Water Purifier Performance Chart breaks down the major categories of pollutants into their specific types. This is important in evaluating purifier performance. For example, on the chart the second vertical column fom the left is for BC (block carbon) filters. Notice how differently the same type of filter performs on viruses and cysts. Breaking down the categories of pollutants in this way gives a clearer picture of what water purifiers can actually do.

Comparing Costs

The Cost Comparison Chart makes several assumptions. First, the purchase prices shown do not include any installation costs. This is because many purifiers don't require any installation— they just snap onto a faucet and are ready to use. If a purifier does require installation, the installation can usually be done by someone who is handy with basic hand tools. If the dealer installs it, expect a cost of $100–200 to be added to the purchase price, depending on the complexity of the installation (many dealers include installation in their prices).

Filters, distillers and ROs come in many varieties, and you can choose one that instantly plugs in or one that requires connecting to your water line. The disadvantage of the instant plug-in purifiers is that they take up counter space and can get in the way of kitchen operations. Installed purifiers, on the other hand, are hidden away under the sink or in a garage or utility room. So it is a matter of spending more money to gain convenience.

The longer a filter cartridge or other replaceable component remains in operation, the lower the per-gallon costs of making drinking water. Because of this, manufacturers stretch their claims about the lifetimes of their products to be able to claim a low cost of operating the unit. However, as I mentioned in Chapter 7, filters should be replaced every six months for optimum performance and safety, regardless of the manufacturer's recommendations. The Cost Comparison Chart is based on this recommendation. In addition, RO membranes and UV lamps are assumed to last for two years, which is their average lifetime.

With the exception of distillers used alone (without filters), all of the recommended water purifiers employ cartridges that must be periodically replaced. Replacement of these cartridges is easy for someone who can use simple hand tools. On the chart, the first column of cost-per-gallon prices (marked "No. 1") applies if you replace cartridges yourself or you can enlist a friend to do it for you without charge. If a dealer is asked to replace them, there will be an extra charge and the cost per gallon of making drinking water goes up. The second column of cost-per-gallon prices ("No. 2") reflects the added charge for a dealer to install all replacement cartridges.

Water Purifier Performance

○ = Complete Removal of Pollutant

● = No Removal of Pollutant

		GC Filter	BC Filter	REDOX + GC Filters	REDOX + BC Filters	BACT. + CARB. Filters	REDOX + BACT. + GC Filters	Batch Distiller
Microorganisms	Bacteria	●	◑	◑	◑	○	○	○
	Viruses	●	●	◑	◑	●	◑	○
	Cysts	●	○	◑	○	○	○	○
Minerals	Toxic metals	●	●	◑	○	●	◑	○
	Nitrates and other non-metals	●	●	●	◑	◑	◑	○
	Asbestos fibers	●	○	◑	●	◑	○	○
Organics	Volatiles	○	○	○	○	○	○	●
	Pesticides, PCBs, herbicides, and other non-volatiles	○	○	○	○	○	○	○
Radioactives	Radon	○	○	○	○	○	○	○
	Uranium and radium, dissolved	●	●	○	○	●	○	○
	Uranium and radium particles	●	◑	○	◑	○	◑	○
Additives	Chlorine	○	○	○	○	○	○	○
	Fluoride	○	○	○	○	○	○	○
	Mineral alkalizers and flocculents	●	●	●	●	●	●	○
	Organic additives	○	○	○	○	○	○	◑
Tastes and smells	Hydrogen sulfide and other volatiles	○	○	○	○	○	○	○
	Dissolved minerals	○	○	○	○	○	○	○
	Mineral and organic particles	◑	●	◑	●	◑	○	○

Abbreviations used:

GC = Granular Carbon
BACT. = Bacteria
REDOX = Reduction-Oxidation Filter
BC = Block Carbon
RO = Reverse Osmosis
CARB. = Carbon Filter
UV = Ultra-Violet

	Water Flow Distiller	Batch Distiller + CARB. Filter	Water Flow Dist. + CARB. Filter	RO + GC Filters	RO + BC Filters	RO + BACT. + CARB. Filters	RO + REDOX + GC Filters	RO + REDOX + BC Filters	RO, REDOX, BACT, + GC Filters	UV	UV + GC Filter	UV + BC Filter	UV + REDOX + GC Filters	UV + REDOX + BC Filters
Bacteria	○	○	○	◐	○	○	◐	○	○	○	○	○	○	○
Viruses	○	○	○	◐	◐	◐	◐	◐	○	○	○	○	○	○
Cysts	○	○	○	○	○	○	○	○	●	●	◐	●	○	○
Toxic metals	○	○	○	◐	◐	◐	◐	◐	●	●	●	●	○	○
Nitrates and other non-metals	○	○	○	◐	◐	◐	◐	◐	●	●	●	●	◐	◐
Asbestos fibers	○	○	○	◐	◐	◐	◐	◐	●	●	◐	◐	◐	◐
Volatiles	◐	○	○	○	○	○	○	○	●	○	○	○	○	○
Pesticides, PCBs, herbicides, and other non-volatiles	○	○	○	○	○	○	○	○	●	○	○	○	○	○
Radon	○	○	○	○	○	○	○	○	●	○	○	○	○	○
Uranium and radium, dissolved	○	○	○	◐	◐	○	○	○	●	●	●	◐	○	○
Uranium and radium particles	○	○	○	○	○	○	○	○	◐	●	◐	◐	○	○
Chlorine	○	○	○	○	○	○	○	○	●	○	○	○	○	○
Fluoride	○	○	○	◐	◐	○	○	○	●	◐	◐	◐	○	○
Mineral alkalizers and flocculents	○	○	○	◐	◐	◐	○	○	●	●	●	◐	◐	○
Organic additives	◐	○	○	○	○	○	○	○	●	○	○	○	○	○
Hydrogen sulfide and other volatiles	○	○	○	○	○	○	○	○	●	○	○	○	○	○
Dissolved minerals	○	○	○	○	○	○	○	○	●	●	●	●	○	◐
Mineral and organic particles	○	○	○	○	○	○	○	○	◐	●	◐	◐	○	○

Notes: 1) All purifier combinations on this chart include a sediment filter as the 1st stage except for the distiller systems, which do not require one.

2) Performance ratings are based on top-performing products only—they do not include all available products.

3) In those systems where a granular or black carbon filter work equally well, the general term "carbon filter" is used.

Cost Comparison of Water Purifiers

Type of Water Purifier	Range of Prices	Cost per Gallon (1) *	Cost per Gallon (2)**
GC Filter	$100–200	$.06–.11	$.14–.24
BC Filter	120–250	.08–.15	.17–.27
REDOX + GC Filters	120–220	.07–.12	.15–.25
REDOX + BC Filters	200–375	.09–.16	.18–.28
BACT. + CARB. Filters	220–400	.13–.22	.21–.35
REDOX + BACT. + GC Filters	230–425	.14–.23	.22–.36
Batch Distiller	120–1200	.25–.40	.25–.40
Water Flow Distiller	300–1200	.22–.35	.22–.35
Batch Distiller + CARB. Filter	175–1200	.29–.44	.40–.62
Water Flow Dist. + Carb. Filter	375–1200	.26–.39	.37–.57
RO + GC Filter	300–600	.11–.20	.19–.33
RO + BC Filter	325–625	.13–.24	.22–.36
RO + BACT. + CARB. Filters	375–700	.18–.31	.26–.44
RO + REDOX + GC Filters	360–700	.12–.21	.20–.34
RO + REDOX + BC Filters	375–700	.14–.25	.23–.37
RO + REDOX + BACT. + GC Filters	500–800	.19–.32	.27–.45
UV	200–700	.12–.16	.19–.28
UV + GC Filter	250–775	.16–.23	.23–.35
UV + BC Filter	275–800	.23–.34	.30–.46
UV + REDOX + GC Filters	350–875	.18–.25	.25–.37
UV + REDOX + BC Filters	375–900	.25–.36	.32–.48

* = cartridge replacement by owner
** = cartridge replacement by dealer

Notes:
1) Purchases prices vary greatly with the particular product selected. The prices shown here do not cover all available products but only the top-performing, *recommended* ones.
2) Installation costs, if any, depend on the particular product selected and on how it is installed. These costs are not included in the purchase prices shown.
3) Costs per gallon assume filters are changed every six months and RO membranes and UV lamps are replaced every two years.

Deciding What To Do About Your Water

Water store?   Buy a purifier?

Bottled water?   Vending machine?

Rent a purifier?   Do nothing?

CHAPTER 10

Previous chapters have described the merits and drawbacks of various kinds of bottled water and the effectiveness and costs of water purifiers. Now you're at the point where you start deciding what to do about your tap water.

Bottled Water Or Purifier?

Since doing nothing about your tap water is not a good option, your first decision is whether to buy some kind of bottled water or make your own drinking water with a purifier. In Chapter 6 I described the different kinds of bottled waters available and which are of the highest quality. In spite of occasional bad publicity, bottled water can be a good solution to obtaining quality drinking water if a bit of care is taken in its selection. Chapters 7, 8 and 9 explained the types of water purifiers available in detail. While many water purifiers on the market do not perform well (some even add more pollutants than they remove), the top-performing purifiers do a good job of removing pollutants.

The Bottled Water vs. Purifiers chart compares the basic performance, convenience and cost of bottled water and purifiers. One point the chart makes is that you can get good-quality drinking water by buying bottled water *or* by buying or renting a water purifier. So the decision rests mostly on cost and convenience differences.

Bottled water is most convenient, of course, when it is home-delivered. There is no lugging of heavy bottles from store to home. But the price per gallon for home-delivered water is higher than for other bottled water. With water purifiers, there is a wide range of convenience factors and a correspondingly wide range of prices.

An important point, which bears repeating, is: You can get high-quality drinking water both from bottled water and from water purifiers. By "high quality," I mean drinking water that is *essentially free of most* known pollutants and is as safe as any of the other food we ingest. However, there are water purifiers available that will go beyond that and remove *essentially all* pollutants from water, and will maintain that performance level consistently and indefinitely. These are the systems that combine distillers and filters.

Bottled Water Vs. Purifiers

Type	Cost	Convenience	Water Quality
Bottled water from stores	$.60-$1.00 per gal.	Inconvenient	Good
Bulk water, delivered	$1.00-$1.75 per gal. plus deposit on dispenser	Very convenient	Good
Bulk water from water stores	$.35-$.50 per gal. plus purchase of empty bottles	Inconvenient	Good
Bulk water from vending machines	$.35-$.50 per gal plus purchase of empty bottles	Inconvenient	Good
Rent a purifier	$15-$40 per month rental fee ($.20-$80 per gal.)	Fairly to very convenient depending on model	Fair to excellent depending on model
Buy a purifier	Initial cost from $100-$1200 plus $.06-$.62 per gal. depending on model	Fairly to very convenient depending on model	Fair to excellent depending on model

If your decision is to buy some kind of bottled water, at this point you may want to review Chapter 6. If you are interested in a water purifier, the remainder of this chapter and all of Chapter 11 are devoted to additional information on purifiers.

How Much Purifier Do You Need?

How much water purification you need depends on how bad your water is. The tap water in some areas contains a plethora of very harmful contaminants, while in others it may be relatively pure, with just small amounts of chlorine and chlorine by-products (THMs). By comparing your Tap Water Profile (page 45) with the Water Purifier Performance chart (pages 106–107), you will get an idea of which kinds of purifiers will provide you with safe drinking water.

Purifier Installations:
What Will Work Best For You?

Some water purifiers, such as portable filters and distillers, are freestanding and don't need to be connected to anything. The simplest hookup is shown in illustration No. 1. This is a counter-top RO or filter with a single tube from the faucet. When the button on a diverter is pushed, water flows to the purifier and out the spigot of the purifier.

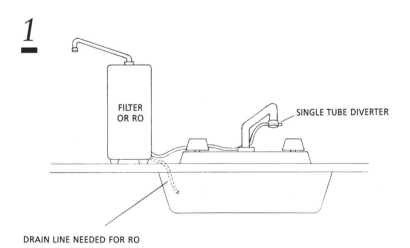

1

FILTER
OR RO

SINGLE TUBE DIVERTER

DRAIN LINE NEEDED FOR RO

In installation No. 2, a countertop filter is connected to the faucet by a double tube. When the button on the diverter is pushed, tap water flows from the faucet to the purifier and treated water returns to the faucet. This is less convenient than No. 1 when you have to fill a large container in the sink.

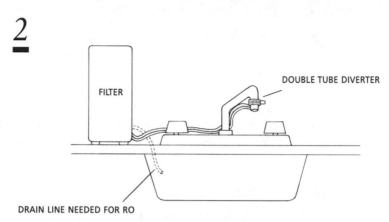

In installation No. 3, a filter is installed under the sink. It receives water from the cold water line and the treated water is connected to a countertop spigot. Undersink installations are the most convenient because there is no purifier to get in the way on the countertop, and no above-sink tubes connect to the sink faucet.

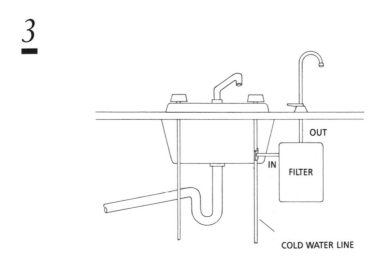

In installation No. 4, an RO is installed under the sink. In addition to the cold water and countertop faucet connections, a drain line directs waste water to the kitchen drain and the output of the RO is connected to a storage tank. When the RO produces water, it fills the storage tank, and enlarges an expandable bladder within the tank. The enlarged bladder exerts pressure on the water going up to the faucet so that water will flow from the faucet at all times.

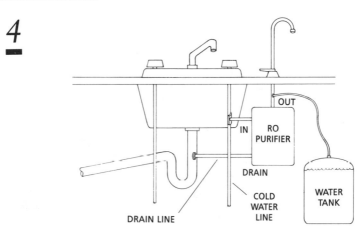

In installation No. 5, an automatic distiller is installed on the countertop. It is connected to the cold water input line and to the drain. An internal storage tank stores distilled water and has its own spigot.

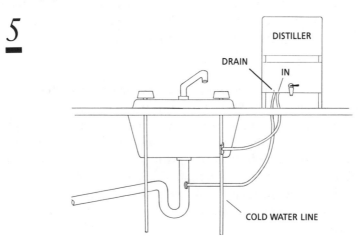

In installation No. 6, an automatic distiller is installed under the sink. It is connected to the cold water input line, to the drain and to a countertop faucet. It has its own built-in storage tank. When the lever on the faucet is pushed, it actuates a small pump (called a *demand* pump because it operates only on demand, when the drinking water faucet lever is pressed) that delivers distilled water to the faucet.

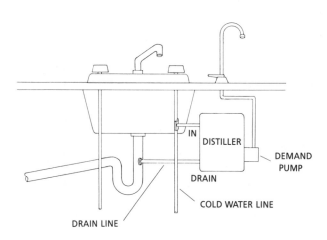

Living With A Water Purifier

Each type of water purifier has its own characteristics, which make it easier or harder to live with. Here are some helpful things to know about before you buy a purifier.

Distiller Characteristics

All distillers generate as much heat as a small portable electric heater, plus humidity. Be aware of this if you will be installing one in a permanent location. Also, batch-type distillers are cooled by a fan, so they are a bit noisy. Most home distillers require three to five hours to make one gallon of distilled water, which means that the fan will remain on for long periods. For permanent installations, it is sometimes a good idea to install the distiller in a garage or other out-of-the-way location and route water tubing to your kitchen.

Distillers require almost no maintenance when the input water has been softened. With hard water, scale builds up and hardens in the boiling chamber, so that it is difficult to clean. Because of this, easy access to the boiling chamber is one of the most important features of a distiller.

Another characteristic of distillers is that the treated water comes out hot. If you are out of drinking water and are waiting for the next batch with bated breath, you will have to wait until the water cools down.

Batch distillers are water-efficient, but water flow distillers waste several times more water than they make. You should consider this if you live in an area where water is scarce.

For all their inconveniences, distiller systems produce the most consistent and reliably safe water of any purification process. The water produced will be as pure after the distiller has given ten or twenty years of service as it was when the distiller was new.

Reverse Osmosis Characteristics

Like distillers, RO's make water very slowly. If you should have a need for several gallons of drinking water at one time, this will empty your storage tank and you will have to wait several hours for the RO to produce more water.

You should also be aware that RO systems degrade and/or foul easily if the tap water exceeds certain limitations (temperature, dirtiness, acidity, etc.) It is absolutely necessary to know the mineral content of your tap water before installing an RO system. *Verify that your dealer knows what is in your water before installing an RO system.*

In general, ROs waste water—some more than others. If you live in an area where water is scarce, check out the recovery rate of the RO you are interested in. Some ROs are very inefficient, with a recovery rate of 1:8 or more (meaning that they waste eight times as much water as they make). More efficient units can have recovery rates as low as 1:2. Also, there is at least one brand of RO that wastes no water at all (see Chapter 11). Some ROs keep making and wasting water even when the storage tank is full. (Several states now have laws requiring RO systems to have automatic shutoff valves that stop the flow of water when there is a full tank.)

RO membranes are delicate and subject to degradation under certain water conditions. I strongly recommend that you be sure any RO you buy includes an output test device. This is a simple electrical meter that measures how efficiently the RO membrane is working. These devices are inexpensive and easy to install. If the RO you are considering does not include one, ask your dealer to add it to your system.

ROs operate on water pressure, and the higher the pressure, the more thorough the rejection of pollutants. Most ROs require at least 40 psi (pounds per square inch) of water pressure for effective operation. The pressure in a typical home is above this, usually 50–70 psi. Low pressure is typically present in an older home where the water pipes are corroded, or on a private water system where the water must be pumped up to a house on a high elevation. Your dealer should check your water pressure before installing an RO system. If the pressure is too low, a miniature booster pump can be added to the RO unit.

As mentioned earlier, there are two types of membranes available for ROs. The first is called a CA membrane (for cellulose acetate). The second type is called a TFC membrane (for thin film composite). The CA type is less expensive, works well on most chlorinated tap water and does a good job of removing pollutants. The TFC type is more expensive (it adds $25–50 to the cost of an RO system). TFCs cannot tolerate chlorinated water (a carbon or redox prefilter is necessary to remove chlorine), but they outperform CA membranes. Where a CA membrane might remove 90–95 percent of most pollutants, a TFC membrane will remove about 97 percent. TFC membranes also last longer. Before you buy an RO system, ask your dealer if a TFC membrane is available, and specify this type if you can when you buy a system.

ROs don't need electricity. This makes them much more energy-efficient than distillers. While a distiller system gives the most thorough removal of all pollutants from water, a good quality RO system is silent, doesn't use electricity or generate heat and humidity, and comes close to a distiller system in effectiveness.

Filter Characteristics

Filters by themselves cannot remove the total spectrum of possible pollutants from water. But good-quality filters can often remove the most harmful pollutants from water, and *filtered water is much better than untreated tap water.* Filters can be relatively inexpensive to buy and inexpensive to operate. In addition, they are more convenient than either ROs or distillers because they produce water—as much as you need—immediately. Because of this there is no need for storage tanks.

Filters come in all shapes, sizes and prices. But there is one type of filter system that has many advantages over all of the others; it is the kind that uses standard, 9¾-inch (sometimes called 10-inch) cartridges. The first advantage of this design is that a wide variety of filter cartridges are available and interchangeable: sediment, granular carbon, block carbon, redox, alumina and bacteria cartridges, to name a few. Because of their interchangeability, you can stack several cartridges together to customize a filter system that will fit your particular needs. Or you can change cartridges at any later date without modifying the system.

Standard filter cartridges are also the best buys. With a nonstandard filter, the replacement innards are usually proprietary— that is, filter replacements are only available from the company that sold the filter. This means that that company can, and usually does, charge a high price for replacements. Standard cartridges, in contrast, are in a highly competitive market and their prices reflect this.

Lastly, the filter housings and fittings for standard cartridge filters are mass-produced and inexpensive. All of this makes for effectiveness, flexibility and good value. While there are many good nonstandard filters on the market, I recommend 9¾-inch standard filter cartridges as the best choice for water purification systems.

Standard 9¾-inch filter cartridges with housing

One optional feature to consider when buying a water filter is a flow meter, which counts the gallons of water produced and turns off the water supply when the filter has processed a specified number of gallons. These are helpful in reminding you to replace filter cartridges. But most of them aren't adjustable—you can't set them for 500 gallons if they are factory-set for 1,000 gallons. Flow meters also add to the price of a water filter. If you are reasonably careful about scheduling cartridge replacements, you may not need this option.

There is a popular type of mini filter on the market that I do not recommend. It is a small, self-contained device that fastens onto the end of a kitchen faucet. These miniature filters do not contain enough carbon for the water flowing through them to have adequate contact time. Their main advantage is that they are relatively cheap, $25–40. If you must use one of these devices, trickle the water through it as slowly as you can and change the small cartridge every month. (The necessity of changing the cartridge so frequently quickly negates the cost advantage of these filters.)

**Mini filters that fit on faucets
are not recommended**

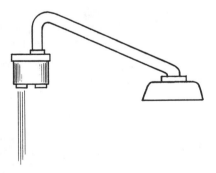

UV Characteristics

Ultraviolet purifiers have a single purpose—to kill bacteria and viruses. UVs have traditionally been used on private water systems that may contain these microorganisms. For this purpose, UVs compete effectively with chlorinators and iodinators that add chlorine or iodine to the water. They also compete with ozonators—devices that generate ozone gas as a disinfectant. For disinfecting water, a UV has a distinct advantage in that it adds no toxic chemicals to the water.

In water vending machines as in other commercial applications, UVs act as the final stage of the purfication process. If there has been any bacterial contamination anywhere in a system, the final UV stage provides the safety backup that disinfects the water.

UV lamps have a limited lifetime—usually one to two years of constant operation. Some units have a lamp-activating feature, so that the lamp turns on only when water is being drawn through the unit. This feature extends the life of the lamp, but eventually all UV lamps have to be replaced. So an important feature of a UV is whether or not the lamp is easy to replace. Also, UV lamps (or the clear quartz covers that protect them) get dirty and must be cleaned occasionally. Some UV units have built-in wiper arms so that the lamp can be cleaned from the outside of the unit, without taking anything apart. Others must be partially disassembled for cleaning. The most important feature of a UV unit is an alarm or shut-off device that operates if the intensity of UV energy falls below a critical level for any reason.

A UV is a specialized device. It doesn't have the ability to remove the wide variety of water pollutants that other types of purifiers do. If you'll refer to the Water Purifier Performance chart on pages 106–107, you will notice that most UV systems show a lot of completely black circles, indicating no removal of that kind of pollutant. In order to remove a wide variety of pollutants, you need to combine a UV with several filters, as in the vertical column on the far right of the chart. And in putting together an effective UV combination, you'll probably spend more money than you would with an alternative system. So when would you want a UV system?

If you are on a private water system that is unchlorinated, UV is one of the surest and safest ways to disinfect your drinking water. If the source for your private system is surface water, you will need a UV system with a block carbon filter or a bacteria filter to trap any possible cysts in the water, which UV does not kill.

UV is also a good solution when your tap water comes from a public water supply that has been disinfected, but there have still been outbreaks of disease from the water. In this case, a UV system would be an effective means of killing waterborne bacteria and viruses. As outbreaks of illness within communities are increasingly traced to waterborne microorganisms, the use of a UV system becomes increasingly attractive.

Purifiers: Should You Buy Or Rent?

Renting a water purifier is not an option in all areas. If you are interested in renting a water purifier, call the dealers in your area to find out if they have rental programs.

Distillers, filters, and UV and RO purifiers may be available for rental. Monthly rental fees average about $20. This should include service calls and the periodic replacement of cartridges. There may be an installation charge. Or, alternatively, you may be required to sign a rental agreement and prepay for six months or so.

The most common rental units are RO systems that come with two filter cartridges—a sediment prefilter and a granular carbon postfilter. To gauge the performance of this combination, refer to the Water Purifier Performance Chart on pages 106–107 and note the performance of the "RO + GC filter" system. This combination does a pretty good job of removing most pollutants. One of its weak points is the removal of nitrates. If you are considering renting this type of purifier, be sure to check with your local water company to see if there are high levels of nitrates in your tap water.

If you do rent an RO system, it is important to monitor the performance of the RO membrane (you usually can't tell what condition it's in by the taste or appearance of the water). This is easly done with a simple electrical test meter. Either the rental unit will have one built in or the dealer will have a service person check it at regular intervals. If the rental unit does *not* have a built-in test meter, the dealer should check the RO membrane at least every six months.

Other types of purifiers can sometimes be rented; ask around to find out what's available in your area. If you are considering renting a distiller, however, you should probably do so only if you can feed the distiller softened water. Hard water causes rapid buildup of scale in a distiller, and frequent (sometimes difficult) cleaning is required.

A rental unit can be a viable option for improving your drinking water. It saves you a large, up-front cash outlay. If you are interested in eventually buying a purifier, renting one allows you to try out a purifier for a while before you invest a larger amount by purchasing it.

Points To Remember
When Choosing A Purifier

Once you have decided what type of purifier best suits your needs, you are ready to look at particular models. All of the water purifiers described in the next chapter will improve your tap water. Here are a few points to remember when choosing one.

- Do *something* about improving your tap water. If you are delayed in getting a purifier, drink a good-quality bottled water until you are able to get one.

- Compare your Tap Water Profile with the performance of purifiers as shown in the Water Purifier Performance chart.

- Don't assume that manufacturers' claims are true—they are often not, even when the dealer sincerely believes them.

- In addition to considering performance and cost, pay attention to convenience. There are a lot of water purifiers stored in closets and garages, unused, because their owners found them to be too much trouble.

- When you have a purifier, maintain it properly and replace cartridges as recommended in this book. An improperly maintained purifier can add more pollutants to the water than are in the untreated tap water.

Selecting A Water Purifier

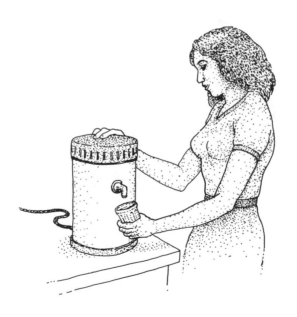

CHAPTER 11

Chapters 7 through 10 described the general characteristics of different types of purifiers—how they work, what pollutants they remove, the advantages and disadvantages of different systems—to help you determine which type of purifier will work best for you and your tap water. This chapter gives you the specific information on manufacturers, models, and options that you will need to decide which particular purifier to purchase.

Filter Systems

The filter systems I recommend all employ standard 9¾-inch cartridges. There are several advantages to this. For one thing, the cartridges, housing and fittings are all interchangeable and easily obtainable. For another, these cartridges are by far the best bargains when replacement is needed. But most of all, the many different kinds of filters made to the 9¾-inch standard allow you geat flexibility in custom-designing a water purifier for your particular needs. This flexibility is not available with any other type of filter.

More than one thousand companies offer these kinds of water filters. Some of them offer single-cartridge purifiers only. Others offer two-, three-, and four-cartridge purifiers. The only significant differences between them are the number of cartridges and the particular type of cartridges used. Some manufacturers sell only one particular combination of cartridges; others offer several alternative cartridges.

It would be impossible to list all of the filter dealers in each area of the United States that sell standard water filters. Rather than attempt this, I have listed, as sources, the manufacturers of these products. When you contact them, they'll be able to tell you the name and location of the dealer nearest you.

Typical single cartridge countertop filter

Typical dual cartridge filter for undersink installation

Single filters cost:	$100–150
Dual filters cost:	$150–250
Triple filters cost:	$250–350

Sources For Standard Water Filters

Alpha Filtrol
Alpha
403 West Main Street
Fountain City, IN 47341

Ametek, Inc.
502 Indiana Avenue
Sheboygan, WI 53082

Aqua Man, Inc.
P.O. Box 3906
Westlake Village, CA 91359

Aquaspace
Western Water
7715 Penn Belt Drive
Forestville, MD 20747

Clean Machine
Aqua Flow, Inc.
6244 Frankford Avenue
Baltimore, MD 21206

Keystone Filter
2385 North Penn Road
Hatfield, PA 19440

Rainsoft Water Conditioning
2080 Lunt Avenue
Elk Grove Village, IL 60007

Trendsetter
Enviroguard, Inc.
260 South Alma School Road
Mesa, AZ 85202

Water Guard
Action Manufacturing &
    Supply Co.
1226 Southeast 9th Terrace
Cape Coral, FL 33990

Watermaster
Ecowater Systems
P.O. Box 64420
St. Paul, MN 55164

Water Purifier
Coastal Industries
Carlstadt, NJ 07072

Water Stand
Plymouth Sales Co.
1115 West Struck Avenue
Orange, CA 92667

Typical 9¾-inch cartridges

Types of cartridges:

- Sediment, pleated
- Sediment, wound
- Sediment, rigid foam
- Granular carbon
- Block carbon
- Bacteria, ceramic

- Bacteria, membrane
- Combination ceramic/carbon
- Combination sediment/carbon
- Redox
- Alumina
- Nitrate

Sources For Standard 9¾-Inch Filter Cartridges

A & C Water Distributors
1000 East Route 34
Plano, IL 60545

Ametek, Inc.
502 Indiana Avenue
Sheboygan, WI 53082

Applied Membranes, Inc.
110 Bosstick Boulevard
San Marcos, CA 92069

Aqua Man, Inc.
P.O. Box 3906
Westlake Village, CA 91359

Clack Corporation
4462 Duraform Lane
Windsor, WI 53598

Di-Tech
590 West Central Avenue #A
Brea, CA 92621

Fibredyne, Inc.
49 Crosby Road
Dover, NH 03820

Matt-Son, Inc.
28W005 Industrial Avenue
Barrington, IL 60010

U.S. Water Products, Inc.
5250 Bonsai Avenue
Moorpark, CA 93021

Water Equipment Technologies
832 Pike Road
West Palm Beach, FL 33411

Reverse Osmosis Systems

Most reverse osmosis purifiers for home use are designed for undersink installation. They typically include an RO membrane cartridge; a sediment prefilter that protects the RO membrane; a carbon postfilter that removes any remaining chemicals and gives the water a good taste; a storage tank for treated water; and a faucet to be installed on the countertop. Some systems come with an extra carbon prefilter for additional protection of the RO membrane. These undersink ROs must be connected to your cold water line and to a drain pipe (as shown in installation No. 4 on page 115).

Like standard filters, these ROs employ standard 9¾-inch filters which are effective, inexpensive, and easy to replace. Some undersink ROs have smaller, nonstandard filters. Since there is little difference in cost, I do not recommend ROs with nonstandard filters because the filters are harder to replace and you do not have the flexibility of easily interchangeable cartridges. For example, if you buy an RO that comes with a standard, granular carbon cartridge, you can easily replace it with a block carbon cartridge and improve the performance of the system.

Standard Undersink RO Systems

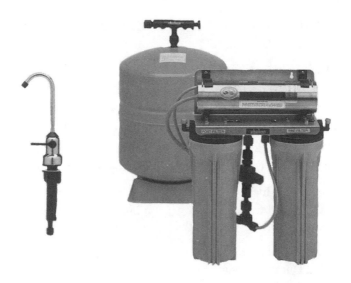

Standard undersink ROs produce 6–20 gallons of purified water in a twenty-four-hour period. This is usually far more than is needed, and the unit is off for most of the day. But the amount of drinking water available at any particular time depends on the size of the storage tank. RO storage tanks typically hold 2–4 gallons of purified water, and this, too, is usually more than enough for an average family's use.

Full-Size Countertop RO Systems

RO systems are also made in a variety of countertop designs which don't require any installation. These connect to a kitchen faucet as shown in Installation No. 1 on page 113, except that an additional drainage tube leads into the sink. Full-size countertop ROs perform about the same as undersink units; some employ standard cartridge filters as part of the unit, while others use smaller filters to achieve a more compact size. Where the undersink units have a separate storage tank, the countertop units have a built-in tank.

Mini RO Systems

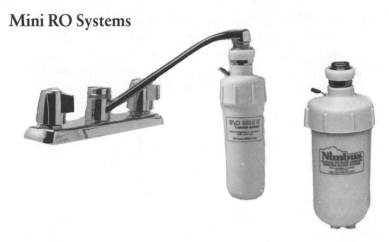

There are also miniature ROs that are inexpensive, take up very little space, and perform surprisingly well. Like the countertop units, these mini ROs require no installation—they snap onto a kitchen faucet. In reverse osmosis, the size of the membrane determines the *quantity* of water produced, not the *quality*. So with a mini RO, the smaller membrane produces less water but the quality of water produced is about as good as with larger units. A weak point of one mini RO is the small carbon postfilter, which wears out quickly and doesn't allow enough water-contact time to be effective.

In contrast to the full-size units, which produce 6–20 gallons per day, a mini RO makes about 3 gallons per day. The mini units don't have storage tanks, and the purified water drips through a small tube into your own container that you place in the sink.

Mini ROs have several limitations, but when available space and cost are limiting factors, they can be of real benefit.

Full-size undersink RO systems cost:	$450–800, installed
Full-size countertop RO systems cost:	$250–350
Mini ROs cost:	$90–175

Recommended Manufacturers For Full-Size Undersink RO Systems

Atlantic Filter Co.
3112 45th Street
West Palm Beach, FL 33407

Challenger Water International
133 Newport Drive #1
San Marcos, CA 92069

Hydrotechnology, Inc.
24844 Anza Drive
Valencia, CA 91355

Nimbus Corporation
288 Distribution Street
San Marcos, CA 92069

Pro Water Systems
2434 East Fender Avenue
Fullerton, CA 92631

Sunburst Water Technologies
1655 North Main Street
Spanish Fork, UT 84660

Universal Aqua Technologies
12207 Los Nietos Road #C
Santa Fe Springs, CA 90607

Viking Water Systems, Inc.
1604 Monrovia Avenue
Newport, CA 92663

Water Equipment Technologies
832 Pike Road
West Palm Beach, FL 33411

Water Factory Systems
68 Fairbanks
Irvine, CA 92718

Water Products International
2058 Beacon Manor Drive
Fort Myers, FL 33907

Recommended Manufacturers For Full-Size Countertop RO Systems

Challenger Water International
133 Newport Drive #1
San Marcos, CA 92069

Delta Aqua, Inc.
14145 Proctor Avenue #17
City of Industry, CA 91746

Onotek Corporation
700 Waverly Avenue
Mamaroneck, NY 10543

Peridott, Inc.
3351 Edward Avenue
Santa Clara, CA 95054

Water Factory Systems
68 Fairbanks
Irvine, CA 92718

Water Products International
2058 Beacon Manor Drive
Fort Myers, FL 33907

Recommended Manufacturers For Mini RO Systems

Ametek Corporation
502 Indiana Avenue
Sheboygan, WI 53082

Nimbus Corporation
288 Distribution Street
San Marcos, CA 92069

High-Output RO Systems

The following manufacturers make countertop RO units that produce purified water more quickly than other ROs available for home use. The various models make 25–100 gallons per day.

Sunburst Water Technologies
1655 North Main Street
Spanish Fork, UT 84660

Trysan Research, Inc.
1122 South State Street
Provo, UT 84606

High-Efficiency RO System

The following manufacturer makes the only RO system currently available that produces purified water with *no* water drained off as waste. It is the most water-efficient RO made.

BioLab, Inc.
P.O. Box 1489
Decatur, GA 30021

High–Mineral Removal RO Systems

The following manufacturers make RO systems with a special deionization stage that *completely* removes toxic minerals and metals from water. This is especially useful in areas where tap water contains high concentrations of nitrates, mercury, lead, or other toxic minerals.

Aquathin Corporation
2800 West Cypress Creek
  Road
Fort Lauderdale, FL 33309

HOH Water Technology
3481 Old Conejo Road #103
Newbury Park, CA 91320

Distiller Systems

In terms of operating a distiller, there are two basic types: manual and automatic. A manual distiller is portable—it isn't connected to anything. You just place it on any level surface and plug it in. When you want to make distilled water, you manually fill the distiller to a predetermined level and turn it on. An external container is needed to collect the distilled water that drips out. When the distiller has used up all of the water in its boiling chamber, it turns itself off. And like all distillation, it is a slow process: manual distillers require from six to eight hours to make a gallon of distilled water.

The strong point of manual distillers is that they are very simple, very dependable and relatively inexpensive. Their weak point is that the ones on the market either have no carbon postfilter or have an inadequate one. This means they remove essentially all pollutants except volatile organics. If you want to use a manual distiller, I recommend that you get a comprehensive test of your tap water and make sure no volatile organics are present. Alternatively, you can run your tap water through a standard carbon filter before distilling it.

An automatic distiller is more complicated, more convenient and more expensive. The distiller must be connected to a cold water input line and to a drain. When the water in its built-in storage tank decreases to a predetermined low level, the distiller turns itself on, fills itself with tap water, and distills enough to refill its tank. Distilled water is available at all times.

Automatic distillers come with built-in storage tanks of varying sizes, typically 4–12 gallons. The tanks are usually made of stainless steel. The larger the storage tank, the more expensive the distiller.

There are two ways to draw water from an automatic distiller: from a spigot mounted on the built-in storage tank or from a special faucet mounted on a countertop. If you prefer the countertop faucet, a small pump is also needed to pressurize the water from the distiller tank up to the faucet. The pump adds to the cost.

Some distillers are only partially automatic—you have to turn them on to get them started. Then they fill themselves with tap water and start distilling. These distillers typically do not have built-in storage tanks, and you must provide the collecting container. When enough water has been produced, either you turn them off manually or a timer does it for you.

All automatic distillers can be combined with carbon filters for thorough removal of *all* pollutants.

Almost all distillers for home use are made of stainless steel. While stainless steel itself is a fairly inert material that does not leach pollutants into water, some stainless steel items are manufactured using a welding process. The seam created by the weld can contribute pollutants to water. Because of this, it is important to have *seamless* stainless steel boiling chambers and storage tanks in distillers.

The following pages contain descriptions of distillers for home use. While filters and RO systems are mostly standardized, each distiller that is manufactured is a unique device with unique characteristics. It's easy to list product specifications, but they don't really tell you what the unit is like on a day-to-day basis. In order to help the potential buyer, I'm including my subjective impressions in the descriptions that follow.

Portable Distiller

WATERWISE 3000

• Makes 1½ gallons in 7 hours

• 700-watt heating element

• Mini carbon filter in spigot

• Average cost: $350

• Collecting bottle included

Waterwise, Inc.
26200 U.S. Highway 27 South
Leesburg, FL 34748
(800) 874-9028

This lightweight countertop distiller has been around for a long time and has proven to be very dependable. It is simple and easy to use. The exterior housing is plastic. Earlier models had an aluminum boiling chamber which was subject to corrosion, but the product is now supplied with a seamless, stainless steel chamber. The fan in this air-cooled distiller is a bit noisier than those in other portable distillers, but the noise is not really bothersome unless you have to stand near the distiller for long periods while it is operating. The weak point of this unit is the very small carbon filter housed inside the hollow spigot. There is enough carbon to provide good-tasting water but not enough to effectively remove volatile chemicals that may be in the distilled water.

Portable Distiller

ECOWATER

* 485-watt model makes
  1 gallon in 8 hours
  585-watt model makes
  1 gallon in 6 hours

* Mini carbon filter in spigot

* Average cost: $130 for low-powered unit; $175 for high-powered unit

Ecowater Systems
1811 Weir Drive #290
Woodbury, MN 55125
(612)731-7027

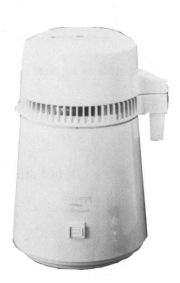

This is the smallest and least expensive distiller available. It is also the slowest in making water because of its small heating element. The unit is air-cooled, dependable, easy to use, and light enough to move anywhere easily. The Ecowater has a plastic housing with a seamless, stainless steel boiling chamber. The tiny carbon filter inside the hollow spigot will improve the taste of the purified water but is not adequate for removing any volatile chemicals that may be in the water.

Portable Distiller

RAIN CRYSTAL

- Only glass distiller made for home use
- Makes 1 gallon every 3 hours
- 1000-watt heating element
- Average cost: $500–600
- Optional carbon postfilter

Scientific Glass Co.
113 Phoenix Avenue Northwest
Albuquerque, NM 87100
(505) 345-7321

This is a very compact, lightweight, water-cooled distiller whose innards are all made of glass and whose design is quite attractive. Laboratory-quality glass is used because it is strong and highly inert, so there is no possibility of water being contaminated by tiny amounts of leaching from the distiller components. The Rain Crystal not only produces very pure distilled water, the whole distillation process is visible and great fun to watch. This little distiller has been around for a long time and in spite of its glass construction is fairly rugged. It is one of the few water-cooled portable distillers made. It is almost completely silent when running and the glass construction reduces heat loss to well below that of most other distillers. However, like all water-cooled distillers, this one wastes water—about 5 gallons for each 1 gallon made. The gravity-drip carbon postfilter that is available as an option enables this distiller to completely remove all contaminants, including volatile chemicals. The Rain Crystal snaps onto a kitchen faucet. It is a semi-automatic distiller; you have to use a collecting container and turn the distiller on manually, and a timer turns it off at a predetermined time.

Portable Distiller

GENESIS 6000

♦ Only "flash" distiller made
for home use

♦ Makes 1 gallon every 3 hours

♦ 1000-watt heating element

♦ Average cost: $350

♦ Removable boiling tray

♦ Two distilled water containers

Genesis Corporation
29 Maxwell Avenue
Toronto, Ontario M5P 2B4
Canada
(416) 488-1345

This is a German-made, air-cooled countertop distiller that has
several unique features. It employs a shallow, two-stage boiling
tray instead of a large boiling container. The water is preheated
in the first tray to remove volatile pollutants, and brought to a
rapid boil in the second tray. This enables the distiller to begin
producing water in only five minutes after being turned on. The
boiling tray is easily removed for cleaning. Two 3-liter (.8-gallon)
glass bottles are provided for distilled water. One can be filled
and placed in a refrigerator while the other is in place for making
more purified water. The glass containers are inert and do not
leach any pollutants into the distilled water. Teabag-sized carbon
filters fit into the necks of the glass bottles. These filters will
improve the taste of the water but are not adequate for removing
any volatile chemicals that remain after preheating the water.
Overall, this is a well-designed, very convenient portable unit.

Air-Cooled Manual And Automatic Distillers

POLAR BEAR

• 1,100-watt models make 1 gallon in 3 hours

• 1,500-watt models make 1 gallon in 2 hours

• Small built-in carbon filter

• Cost: $500–1,200, depending on models and options

Polar Bear Water Distillers
Box 113
Pickardville, Alberta TOG 1WO
Canada
(403) 349-4872

Polar Bear distillers are extremely well-built, dependable air-cooled, manual and automatic distillers that are constructed of all stainless steel. These units have a small, built-in carbon filter that is larger than the tiny spigot filters in portable distillers, but this filter is still inadequate for effectively removing volatile chemicals. The boiling tank is awkward to clean because of a small access lid. Several useful options are available, including different sizes of stainless steel storage tanks and sight gauges for viewing the water level in the tank. A unique feature is that the Polar Bear's storage tanks are protected from possible contamination by airborne bacteria with a special air filter.

Air-Cooled Manual And Automatic Distillers

PURE WATER

* 700- to 1,650-watt heating elements

* Optional storage tanks of several capacities

* Average cost: $500–1,200, depending on options and models

Pure Water, Inc.
3725 Touzalin Avenue
Lincoln, NE 68507
(402) 467-9300

Pure Water, Inc. has been making distillers for a long time, and manufactures a complete line of dependable, well-built units of all stainless steel. Manual and automatic models are available. The small access lid on all models makes cleaning the boiling chamber awkward. Options include a pump for remote installation, various sizes of storage tanks, and sight gauges for checking the level of water in the tank.

Air-Cooled Manual And Automatic Distillers

DURASTILL

* 1,000- and 1,500-watt heating elements

* Optional storage tanks of several capacities

* Average cost: $500–1,200, depending on options and models

Durastill, Inc.
4200 Birmingham Road
Kansas City, MO 64117
(816) 454-5260

Durastill has been making a wide range of manual and automatic distillers for many years. They are of all stainless steel, very dependable and well built. A small access lid makes cleaning the boiling chamber awkward. Sight gauges for determining water level in the tank, demand pumps for remote installation and other options are available.

Air-Cooled
Automatic Distiller

WATERWISE 7000

* Makes 1 gallon every 3 hours

* 1,200-watt heating element

* Average cost: $700–1,200, depending on options

* Optional pre- and postfilters

Waterwise, Inc.
26200 U.S. Highway 27 South
Leesburg, FL 32748
(800) 874-9028

This is an extremely well-designed and well-built distiller. It has an easily removable boiling chamber, which eliminates the awkward cleaning problem common to other distillers. Another unique design feature is a gravity-sensing on-off switch under the boiling chamber. Where other distillers turn off power to the heating element by sensing a temperature rise when the boiling chamber runs out of water, this unit weighs the boiling chamber and turns the power off when the water reaches a minimum level. The advantage of this is that the boiling chamber never completely empties, which reduces scale buildup and helps to protect the heating element. The Waterwise 7000 offers standard, cartridge-type pre- and postfilters as options. With the filters installed, this system is one of the most thorough at removing *all* potential water pollutants. **Highly recommended.** This system is also available under the trade name **Dol-Fyn.**

Air-Cooled
Automatic Distiller

APOLLO

+ Makes 1 gallon every 2 hours

+ 1,500-watt heating element

+ Average cost: $800–1,200, depending on options

+ Several options, including pre- and postfilters

International Water
  Technologies
2200 West Adams
Lincoln, NE 68524
(800) 628-2637

This is a new, thoughtfully designed distiller with a number of
innovative features that have
been lacking on distillers made
for home use. It includes a post-distillation calcium feeder, which
replaces health-promoting minerals lost in the distillation process; an insulated boiling chamber, which makes the Apollo the
most efficient of air-cooled distillers; and a scale-sensing device
that shuts down the unit before scale buildup can damage the
components. All hot components are placed away from external
surfaces so that the distiller covers remain cool and safe for children. It also has unique overheating and flooding protection, and
a removable boiling chamber. **Highly recommended,** and a good
value for the features included. (The company has also developed
a combination distiller–hot water heater that uses the heated
water to also make purified drinking water; contact the company
for details.)

Water-Cooled Automatic Distiller

AR SYSTEMS

* Makes 1 gallon every 2⅔ hours

* 1,000-watt heating element

* Average cost: $900–1,200

* Optional pre- and postfilters

AR Systems, Inc.
111 Terminal Street
Hopewell, VA 23860
(804) 541-8802

This well-made, all-stainless-steel distiller is designed to install under a kitchen sink. Because it is water-cooled, it runs silently and gives off minimal heat and humidity. The price paid for this is that, like all water-cooled distillers, it wastes water—about 4–5 gallons for every gallon of distilled water produced. The boiling chamber is accessible through a large, removable lid. Optional pre- and postfilters are available. With filters installed, this system is one of the most thorough at removing *all* potential pollutants from water.

Water-Cooled
Automatic Distiller

H₂Only

• **Makes 1 gallon every 2 hours**

• **1200-watt heating element**

• **Average cost: $750**

DEW Enterprises
4037 Boone Road
Benton, AR 72015
(800) 467-1030

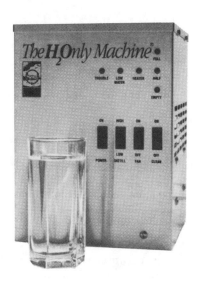

This distiller is a newly introduced product. It is semi-automatic —you turn it on and off and it does the rest. The unit is well built and employs solid-state electrical controls for long life. This distiller is very efficient; it produces an above-average amount of distilled water for the electricity consumed. A nice design feature is a boiling chamber that is removable for easy cleaning. Post-distillation venting plus a built-in post-distillation carbon filter together eliminate any volatile chemicals that may be in the water.

Water-Cooled
Automatic Distiller

AQUAFIER

* Makes 1 gallon in 3½ hours

* 1,000-watt heating element

* Average cost: $900–1,100

Conklin Company
889 Valley Park Drive
Shakopee, MN 55379
(612) 445-6010

This is a compact, fully automatic unit that can be installed on a wall or countertop or under the kitchen sink. Like all water-cooled distillers, it runs quietly and gives off a minimum amount of heat and humidity to the surroundings. Also like all water-cooled distillers, it connects to a cold water line and to a drain, and it drains about 5 gallons of tap water for every gallon of distilled water made. A removable boiling chamber makes cleaning easy. The Aquafier comes with a large sediment prefilter and a moderately large carbon postfilter. This combination of distiller and filter will eliminate *all* potential pollutants from tap water.

Water-Cooled
Automatic Distiller

HYDRO-CLEAN

* Makes 1 gallon every two hours

* The only fractional distiller currently available for home use

* Very compact design

* Average cost: $600–1,200, depending on options

Hague Quality Water
4343 South Hamilton Road
Groveport, OH 43125
(614) 836-2195

In terms of the distillation process itself, the Hydro-Clean is the most sophisticated distiller available for home use. Like all water-cooled distillers, the Hydro-Clean runs quietly and gives off a minimum amount of heat, but wastes water. It employs a vertical steam tube that separates volatile pollutants from steam and vents them off. (This is called *fractional* distillation because it separates evaporating substances into parts, or fractions.) Specially designed baffles in the Hydro-Clean also help to eliminate pollutants and maintain the purity of the distilled water. While the Hydro-Clean, by itself, does eliminate more volatiles than other distillers, that removal may not be total. For complete removable of all volatiles, the Hydro-Clean also includes a granular carbon prefilter. The basic distiller unit has a built-in 1½ gallon tank, which is too small to hold enough water for average use. And because the tank is positioned right over the boiling chamber, the purified water stays warm to hot much of the time. A larger, free-standing tank is available as an option. The optional tank eliminates these problems.

Ultraviolet Systems

There are different reasons for using a UV for water treatment in the home. The first reason is when a water source is known to be contaminated by bacteria and/or viruses. In this case, a whole-house UV is needed. That is, the UV must completely disinfect all of the water that enters the house. And since an entire household can use a large amount of water, UVs required for this purpose are elaborate and relatively expensive—they start at about $1,000 and go up. The second reason for using a UV is on tap water that is free of obvious contamination but may contain small amounts of microorganisms that are potentially harmful when ingested. In other words, to insure that drinking water is safe. A water source known to be contaminated by microorganisms requires improvements that are beyond the scope of this book. Here we are concerned with the second situation, in which UVs are used for drinking water only.

Like distillers, small UVs for drinking water treatment are all different from one another. There are so many different designs that it's easy to get overwhelmed. To help simplify things, I divide UVs into two groups. The first group includes the traditional kinds of UVs—the ones that are housed in stainless steel or other metal and that have lots of built-in features. Some of these units have built-in viewing ports, wiper arms that clean the UV lamp from the outside, UV intensity monitors, temperature monitors, audible alarms and so on. The illustration of traditional UVs shows the various shapes and sizes these units come in.

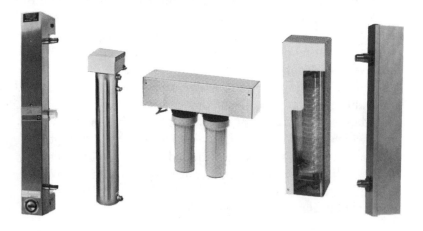

Traditional UVs

Traditional UVs are not cheap. They typically cost from $500 to $700. When filters are added (as they must be if you want removal of other pollutants as well), the cost can climb to $900 or more. To give them their due credit, these UVs are all well-designed, well-built products that are made to last.

Recommended Manufacturers
For Traditional UV Purifier

Atlantic Ultraviolet Corp.
26 North Fehr Way
Bay Shore, NY 11706
(516) 586-5900

Epco Technologies, Inc.
54 Central Street
Fayville, MA 01745
(508) 624-7478

Ideal Horizons
P.O. Box 1707
Rutland, VT 05701
(802) 773-4346

Matt-Son, Inc.
28W005 Industrial Avenue
Barrington, IL 60010
(708) 628-8766

Northfield Products
4053-C Wayside Lane
Carmichael, CA 95608
(916) 973-8465

Trojan Technologies, Inc.
845 Consortium Court
London, Ontario N6E 2S8
Canada
(519) 685-6660

Ultra Dynamics Corp.
1631 10th Street
Santa Monica, CA 90404
(213) 450-6461

Water Conditioning, Inc.
1075 South Batesville Road
Greer, SC 29651
(803) 848-4366

Water Soft, Inc.
220 Ohio Street
Ashland, OH 44805
(419) 289-0633

Recently, a new breed of UV has come on the market. Based on the convenient fact that standard filter cartridges all have an empty hole inside the cartridge that runs its full length, these UV lamps fit right inside of the filter cartridges and use the standard, low-cost filter housing as the housing for the UV as well. This is a terrifically clever way to save money and to match a UV purifier with the best filters available. While traditional UVs cost about

$500–700 plus another $100–200 for filters, these new cartridge-based UVs can be purchased for under $200, or for $300 with filters. This is a real cost breakthrough, and it makes UV purification more useful and appealing. Low-cost add-on UVs are also now available. These can be added to an existing water purifier. For example, RO systems are generally not suitable for private, unchlorinated water systems—bacteria in the water eventually foul the RO membrane. By adding a small UV cartridge in front of the RO, the problem of fouling is eliminated.

Cartridge-Style UV Purifiers

The following company offers an extensive line of low-cost, cartridge-style UV purifiers:

> Pura, Inc.
> 1140 South Aviation Drive
> Provo, UT 84601
> (801) 377-4200

The following companies currently offer limited models of low-cost UV purifiers:

> Ultra Dynamics Corporation
> 1631 10th Street
> Santa Monica, CA 90404
> (213) 450-6461

> Selecto, Inc.
> 2258 Northwest Parkway #A
> Marietta, GA 30067
> (800) 635-4017

UV within a standard filter cartridge

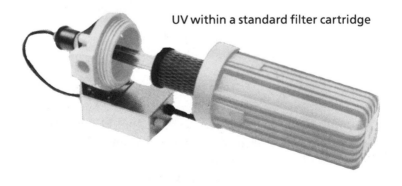

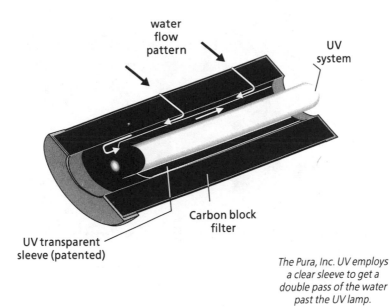

water
flow
pattern

UV
system

Carbon block
filter

UV transparent
sleeve (patented)

*The Pura, Inc. UV employs
a clear sleeve to get a
double pass of the water
past the UV lamp.*

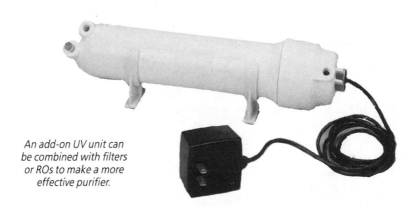

*An add-on UV unit can
be combined with filters
or ROs to make a more
effective purifier.*

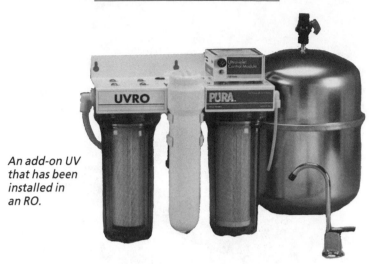

An add-on UV that has been installed in an RO.

Putting Together Your Own System

You can't (conveniently) build your own distiller or manufacture your own ultraviolet purifier but you can save a lot of money by combining standard, readily available components to make up your own water purification system. This also gives you the utmost flexibility in designing an effective system. The components are simple enough that almost anyone who can use common hand tools can assemble them. Here are some of the top manufacturers of components. Contact them for the distributor nearest you.

Filter Housings and Cartridges

Ametek, Inc.
502 Indiana Avenue
Sheboygan, WI 53082
(414) 457-9435

Keystone Filter
2385 North Penn Road
Hatfield, PA 19440
(800) 822-1963

Plymouth Sales Co.
1115 West Struck Avenue
Orange, CA 92667
(714) 997-5482

U.S. Water Products, Inc.
5250 Bonsai Avenue
Moorpark, CA 93021
(805) 523-0198

Water Equipment Technologies
832 Pike Road
West Palm Beach, FL 33411
(305) 684-6300

RO Components, Testers
And Partially Assembled Systems

PJD Associates
22-H North Milpas Street
Santa Barbara, CA 93103
(800) 234-6322

Sprite Industries
2512-B East Fender Avenue
Fullerton, CA 92631
(714) 992-2145

Faucets And Fittings

Lead-Free Faucets, Inc.
P.O. Box 1068
Aurora, OH 44202
(800) 228-4038

Water Scout, Inc.
Box 103
Plymouth, CT 06782
(203) 879-3030

Touch-Flo Manufacturing
59 East Orange Grove Avenue
Burbank, CA 91502
(800) 223-0490

Waterwise, Inc.
26200 U.S. Highway 27 South
Leesburg, FL 32748
(800) 874-9028

CHAPTER 12

Specialty Products And Accessories

CHAPTER 12

Accessories that commonly form a part of a water purifier are listed in Chapter 11. These include RO membrane testers, flow meters that tell how much water has gone through a purifier, faucets and fittings. This chapter includes bottles, water dispensers and other products that may be of interest to readers.

Bottles, Dispensers And Pumps

Good quality water bottles are sometimes hard to find. Most water bottles now sold are made of a clear, blue-tinted plastic called polycarbonate. These are strong, long-lasting and sufficiently inert (they don't leach chemicals into the water for most drinking water uses). Polycarbonate bottles are available in two-, three-, and five-gallon sizes. The smaller sizes are much handier for pouring and carrying.

For distilled water, glass bottles are recommended but are hard to find. A possible source is your local bottled water company that delivers water to homes. These companies sometimes sell their excess five-gallon glass bottles.

There are several models of miniature pumps available that fit onto the necks of water bottles. These enable you to draw water from a water bottle that is standing upright without having to tip the bottle for pouring. Manually operated pumps have a plunger that you have to move up and down, like a bicycle air pump. Battery-driven pumps do it for you.

Ceramic and plastic dispensers that support upside-down water bottles are also available. Push-button or spring-lever spigots release the water.

Water bottles, dispensers and pumps are often sold at stores that sell bulk water and/or purifiers. If you can't find any of these products, here are some companies who make them (and sell them by the case).

Marvel-Tek
5331 Irwindale Avenue
Irwindale, CA 91706
(818) 337-0223

Pure Drinking Water Systems
500 73rd Avenue Northeast
Minneapolis, MN 55432
(800) 637-8731

Presto-Tek
2909 Tanager Avenue
Los Angeles, CA 90040
(800) 421-8660

Pure Systems
1620 Gobel Way
Modesto, CA 95351
(209) 538-6030

Travel Filters For Treated Water

For those who don't want to drink tap water while away from
home, several small, portable water filters are available. These
are for use with treated, uncontaminated tap water—not with
untreated water from lakes, streams and ponds. Let's first dis-
pense with the sipping filters, the small, tubular filters that look
like fat straws. These filters clog easily, they are easily contaminated by bacteria in the mouth, and the fluctuating pressure
within them that is generated by sipping can cause pollutants to
break away and exit with the water. I do not recommend using
any sipping filter.

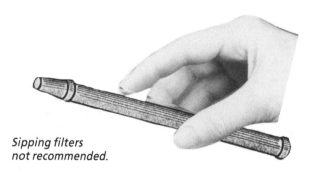

*Sipping filters
not recommended.*

Several multi-piece filters are available. One of the most
popular is a device that has several separate sections which fit
together into the size of a large cup. This filter contains a redox
medium plus granular carbon. The redox medium strongly
inhibits bacterial growth within the filter. Nevertheless, I recommend that, when possible, you store the filter in a refrigerator to

slow the growth of any microorganisms that may be present. To find out how to buy this filter, contact the manufacturer:

International Aqua, Inc.
2662 Aero Drive
Grand Prairie, TX 75051
(214) 988-9090

Pouring cup

Travel filter for treated water

Funnel

Filter

Drinking cup

Camping And Travel Filters For Untreated Water

These filters are very handy if you're camping near an untreated water source or if you're traveling to a foreign country where the water may not be safe. The traditional filters for this purpose employ a dense ceramic medium whose pores are tiny enough to prevent bacteria from getting through. In addition, a silver compound is integrated with the ceramic medium. This helps prevent bacterial growth from extending into the pores of the ceramic and it kills or renders inactive any viruses in the water (unlike silver in a carbon filter, which is not very effective).

I can't resist adding a bit of folklore here. In Europe, it has been a tradition for hundreds of years to place a *silver* coin in a pot of drinking water, for good luck. Perhaps the antibacterial quality of silver was known in the past, and was then forgotten except in this tradition of the silver bringing good luck.

A nice feature of ceramic filters is that the surface of the ceramic can be scrubbed periodically and the filters used for very long periods without replacement.

A newer type of disinfecting filter for untreated water employs a microfilter to trap cysts and parasites, plus an iodine resin medium. In this medium, iodine, which is a powerful disinfectant, contacts the water and instantly kills all remaining microorganisms but does not enter the water because it is tightly bonded to the resin. This is a very effective way to kill all microorganisms in water without contaminating the water with iodine.

The ceramic-silver and iodine resin filters each have advantages. The ceramic type has been around for several decades and has a long track record of providing safe drinking water. While the iodine resin must be replaced after a certain quantity of water has been treated, the ceramic filter can be used indefinitely. This becomes important if you're in a remote area for an extended time and you can't get replacements. On the other hand, the iodine resin filter has a more powerful disinfecting action and *may* be more effective in killing viruses. However, *both the ceramic-silver and iodine resin filters provide safe drinking water from untreated sources.*

The best of the ceramic-silver filters is the Katadyn. For information on Katadyn filters, contact:

Katadyn U.S.A.
3020 North Scottsdale Road
Scottsdale, AZ 85251
(602) 990-3131

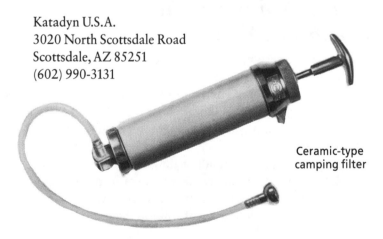

Ceramic-type
camping filter

A nicely designed and well-built product that uses the iodine resin system is the PUR Antimicrobial Water Purifier. It is very compact, has a pressure plunger that forces the water evenly through the filter medium, and includes a spigot that opens up for filling a glass with treated water. **Highly recommended** for travel and camping. For information, contact:

Recovery Engineering, Inc.
2229 Edgewood Avenue South
Minneapolis, MN 55426
(800) 845-7873

Iodine-type camping filter

An innovative product that employs iodine resin is the Purijug filter/container. This is a collapsible plastic water jug that holds up to two gallons and has a built-in disinfecting filter. This is very handy because you don't have to disinfect water cup-by-cup—you can treat and store two gallons at a time. For more information on this product, contact:

Krudico, Inc.
308 East 4th Street
Auburn, IA 51433
(712) 688-2284

In reviewing and testing different products, I have come across all kinds—good and bad. Recently I found a good one that doesn't have too much to do with harmful pollutants in drinking water, but it is such a good idea that it deserves mention.

Those of you who are on private water systems and have dirty water have probably been changing sediment filters for years. Here's a new kind of filter called the Spin-Down. Dirt in the water is separated by centrifugal action and collects at the bottom of the filter. You can see the dirt accumulation through the clear housing. When the dirt builds up, you simply open a valve at the bottom of the housing and it flows out. There is no down time—you don't have to turn off the water to clean the unit. A reusable filter screen is occasionally removed for washing. For information on this product, contact:

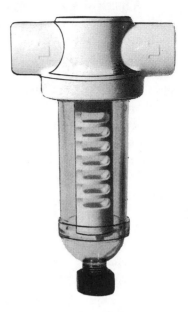

Centrifugal sediment filter

Rusco
13360 Chambord Street
Brooksville, FL 34613
(800) 345-1033

A *R*ADON
*S*UPPLEMENT

A Radon Supplement

(For Households with a High Risk of Radon in the Air and/or Water)

Radon is proving to be the most potentially harmful of any water pollutant. The health hazards it presents are described in Chapter 2, and the removal of radon *from drinking water* by various methods of water purification is described in Chapters 7 through 11. As these chapters explained, however, consuming radon in drinking water is not the greatest threat; inhalation of it and absorption of it through the skin are more serious dangers.

How does radon get into the air in a house? Two ways. It can seep up through the ground and into the basement or foundation and spread through the rest of the house. In this case, radon gas must be prevented from getting into the house and any radon already present must be removed from the air in the house. The remedies for this have to do with modifications to the foundation, air circulation, and so on, and are beyond the scope of this book. Many instructive articles have already been written on this subject.

The second way radon gets into the air in a house is when it enters through the water and evaporates into the air inside the house. In this case, the radon needs to be removed from the water before the water enters the house.

You can have your house tested for radon in the air or in the water for $10–35 per test. This is a one-time test and does not account for any seasonal fluctuations. Most cities have companies that do one-time tests. If you can't find one in your area, or if you want to buy a continuous-monitoring radon tester (costing anywhere from $200 to $1,000), here are some firms that provide one-time radon tests, continuous-monitor testers, or both.

K. G. Cooper & Associates
P.O. Box 14747
Houston, TX 77221

Pineda Products, Inc.
415-C Pineda Court
Melbourne, FL 32940
(407) 259-6862

Rad Elec, Inc.
5330-J Spectrum Drive
270 Technology Park
Frederick, MD 21701
(301) 694-0013

Threshold Technical Products
11325 Reed Hartman Highway
Cincinnati, OH 45241
(800) 458-4931

Test for radon in the air first. If there is a high concentration of radon in the air in your house, further testing of air and water will be needed. If the air in your house is relatively free of radon (radon is present to some degree everywhere), you don't need to test your water.

Test results are measured in pCi/l (picocuries per liter). *The Environmental Protection Agency recommends corrective action if radon in air is 20 pCi/l or higher, and if radon in water is 10,000 pCi/l or more* (although the latter action level will probably drop to 2,000 pCi/l or less in the near future).

If the radon concentration in your water is high (more than 2,000 pCi/l), you should remove it by carbon filtration or by aeration. The type of carbon filter needed to remove radon from all of the water coming into a house is very different from a drinking water filter. A whole-house filter is about the size of a water softener and contains 1½ to 2 cubic feet of granular carbon. Whole-house carbon filters are available through almost all water conditioning dealers. They usually cost about $1,200 plus installation, and the carbon medium lasts about two to three years before it has to be replaced. Replacement costs are about $150 (including cleaning out the tank and installing the fresh carbon). Whole-house carbon filters typically remove about 90 percent of the radon in water.

Whole-house
carbon filter
for radon removal

A low-cost way to partially reduce radon from household water is to install small carbon filters on the showerheads. This won't eliminate radon that evaporates from baths, cooking, and the washing machine, but it will eliminate it from one area within the house that generates high radon concentrations.

Showerhead filters are usually available through water purification dealers. Some shower filters are filled exclusively with a redox medium (which removes chlorine more efficiently than carbon does), but redox can't remove radon. *So if you buy a showerhead filter for radon removal, be sure it includes carbon in its filtering medium.*

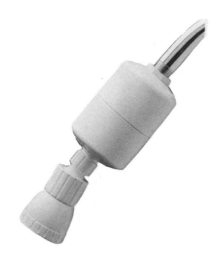

showerhead filter

Atmospheric aeration is expensive, but it is the most effective and safest way to remove radon from water. (Aeration is described in detail in Chapter 7.) Aerators for removing radon can be installed in a basement, garage or utility room with a vent for removing radon (or, where pipes don't freeze, outside the house, with no venting needed). They typically cost about $2,000, including installation.

A private water system with an existing outdoor holding tank already has a potential aerator. You can aerate the water quite effectively simply by installing a fine spray nozzle where the water flows into the tank.

A final note: The Environmental Protection Agency is considering making it mandatory for all public water systems with high concentrations of radon in the water to aerate the water before it can be delivered to homes. As of this writing, there is no timetable for enforcing this.

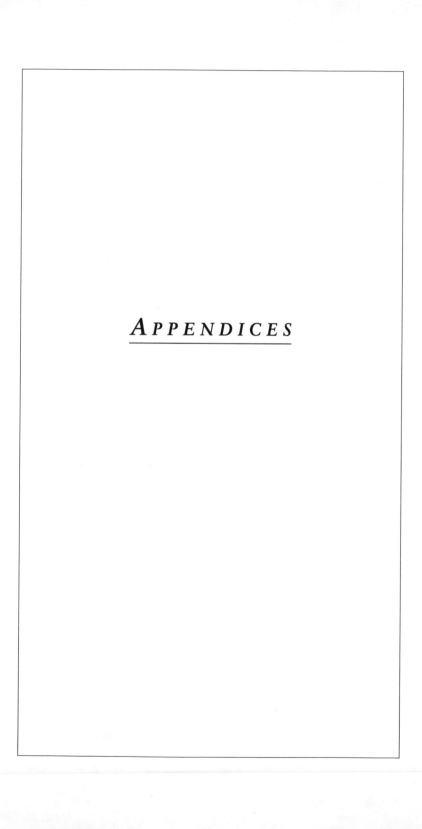

APPENDICES

APPENDIX A

Glossary Of Water Purification Terms

absolute filter rating   Refers to the smallest particle size that a filter will trap 100 percent. For example, a 5-micron *absolute* filter will trap *all* particles 5 microns and larger. See *nominal filter rating*.

activated carbon   Carbon that has been specially treated to enhance its ability to trap certain chemicals.

adsorption   The process by which carbon filters trap chemicals.

aeration   The process of exposing water to large amounts of oxygen in order to remove certain kinds of chemicals.

aggressive water   Water that, because of its purity, aggressively reacts (chemically) with materials it contacts.

aquifier   A naturally occurring underground reservoir.

backwashing   Reversing the flow of water through a filter in order to cleanse it of accumulated particulate matter.

CA membrane   Cellulose acetate membrane. A type of membrane used in reverse osmosis.

carcinogen   A substance that causes or contributes to the onset of cancer.

chloramine   A combination of chlorine and ammonia used to disinfect water.

chlorine   A chemical used to disinfect water.

colloid   A tiny particle that remains in suspension in a liquid.

condensate   Water that has been vaporized and then returned to liquid form. Same as *distillate*.

contact time   The amount of time that water contacts a filter medium while flowing through a filter.

contaminate   A substance in water that is harmful or otherwise undesirable. Same as *pollutant*.

corrosion   A chemical process by which water attacks metal surfaces and weakens or destroys them.

de-ionization (DI)   A process that removes minerals from water by ion exchange.

disinfection   The process of killing bacteria and other micro-organisms in water.

dissolved solids   Particles that have dissolved in water and are in solution. See *total dissolved solids*.

distillate   Water that has been vaporized by boiling and then returned to liquid form. Same as *condensate*.

distillation   The process of boiling water, capturing the steam, and cooling it so that purified water is produced.

effluent   The water flow that exits from a device or system.

feed, feedwater   A solution that enters a device or system for a specific purpose, as in a chlorine feeder.

filtrate   In a treatment device, the water flow after it has passed through a filter or membrane.

finished water   Water that has been improved by a water treatment plant and is ready to be delivered to customers.

flocculent   A substance that is added to water to make particles clump together in order to achieve better filtration.

giardia   A microorganism that occurs in water in the form of cysts; a cause of gastrointestinal disorders.

gpm, gph, gpd   The rate of water flow in gallons per minute, per hour, or per day.

ground water   Water whose source is *underground*.

hardness   The amount of calcium and magnesium in water, which causes it to clean inefficiently.

heavy metals   The toxic metals in water, such as cadmium, lead and mercury.

hydrogen sulfide   A toxic gas in water that smells like rotten eggs.

influent   The water flow input to a device or a system.

ion   An electrically charged atom.

ion exchange   A process by which undesirable ions in water are exchanged for more beneficial ones.

leaching   The process by which chemicals from the walls of a container enter the water in the container.

MCL Maximum contaminant level; the maximum level recommended by federal law for a particular water pollutant.

MCLG Maximum contaminant level goal; the optimum maximum contaminant level in the future, for a particular water pollutant.

membrane A thin material that is porous enough to reject pollutants while allowing pure water to pass through.

mg/l Milligrams per liter. A measure of the amount of a substance in water. The equivalent to parts per million.

micron A shortened term for one micrometer. One millionth of a meter.

mutagen A substance that causes or contributes to genetic mutation.

NDWR National Drinking Water Regulations, as established by the Safe Drinking Water Act of 1974.

NOC Naturally occurring organic chemical.

nominal filter rating Refers to the smallest particle size that a filter will trap *most* of. For example, a 5-micron *nominal* filter might trap 95 percent of all particles 5 microns or larger. See *absolute filter rating*.

oxidizing filter A filter that removes pollutants from water by chemical reaction.

ozone A toxic form of oxygen that is used to disinfect water.

particulate Particles in water.

permeate That portion of the water that passes through an RO membrane.

pH The measure of alkalinity/acidity in water. A pH of 1 to 7 is acidic, 7 to 14 is alkaline, and exactly 7 is neutral.

pollutant A substance in water that is harmful or otherwise undesirable. Same as *contaminant*.

pore size This refers to the smallest substance that an RO membrane will reject *most* of. For example, a .001-micron membrane might reject approximately 90 percent of all substances .001 microns and larger.

PPB Parts per billion. A measure of the amount of a substance in water. One part per billion is equivalent to one $\mu g/l$, or one billionth of a gram per liter.

PPM   Parts per million. A measure of the amount of a substance in water. Equivalent to milligrams per liter (mg/l).

Primary Regulations   National Drinking Water Regulations that pertain to harmful water pollutants.

psi   Pounds per square inch of water pressure.

recovery rate   The ratio of pure water produced to total water used in the process of reverse osmosis.

regeneration   A process by which a filter medium is cleansed of accumulated pollutants, such as by reversing the flow of water through it.

rejection   The process whereby certain substances cannot pass through a membrane and are drained off.

resin   A specially prepared mineral that is used in de-ionization and in some kinds of filters.

reverse osmosis (RO)   A process by which contaminants are rejected by a membrane while pure water is allowed to pass through.

scale   A hard, whitish buildup of mineral deposits on surfaces that contact water, such as the inside of water pipes or the boiling chamber of a distiller.

Secondary Regulations   National Drinking Water Regulations that pertain to the aesthetic and convenience qualities of water.

SOC   Synthetic organic chemical.

softness   The quality of water, desirable for efficient cleaning and minimal corrosion, that results from very low amounts of calcium and magnesium.

teratogen   A substance that causes or contributes to birth defects.

TDS   Total dissolved solids. The standard measure of minerals dissolved in water.

TFC membrane   Thin film composite membrane. A type of membrane used in reverse osmosis.

THM   Trihalomethane. A type of toxic chemical, commonly formed when organic chemicals in water combine with chlorine.

turbidity   A measure of the opacity, or cloudiness of water that is caused by particulates.

ultraviolet disinfection (UV)   A process by which intense ultraviolet light is used to kill bacteria and other micro-organisms.

VOC   Volatile organic chemical. A class of chemicals that evaporate easily and which can be absorbed through the skin.

APPENDIX B

References And Further Reading

For general information:

Environmental Protection Agency hotline: (800) 426-4791. Or write to Environmental Protection Agency, Office of Drinking Water, 401 M Street Southwest, Washington, D.C. 20460.

On water quality:

Council on Environmental Quality. *Annual Report: Environmental Quality*. Washington, D.C.: Government Printing Office, December 1980.

Environmental Protection Agency. *A Drop to Drink: A Report on the Quality of Our Drinking Water*. Washington, D.C.: Government Printing Office, 1976.

_____ . *National Assessment of Rural Water Conditions*, Executive Summary. Washington, D.C.: Government Printing Office, June 1984.

Ingram, Colin. *Water Contamination—A National Problem*. Monterey, CA: Monterey Pacific Institute, 1984.

King, Johnathan. *Troubled Waters: The Poisoning of America*. Emmaus, PA: Rodale Press, 1985.

Public Health Service, Bureau of Water Hygiene. *Community Water Supply Study*. Washington, D.C.: Government Printing Office, 1969.

Shaefer, J., and L. Stevens. *Future Water*. New York: Morrow & Co., 1984.

Silberman, M. "How Well Is the Water?" *Friends of the Earth Newsletter* (San Francisco), October 1984.

On government policy for drinking water:

Environmental Protection Agency. *National Primary Drinking Water Regulations* (various), 1977–1984.

National Academy of Sciences. *Decision Making for Regulating Chemicals in the Environment.* Washington, D.C., 1975.

U.S. Congress: *Safe Drinking Water Act of 1974*, 300f to 300j–9. Public Law No. 93–523.

On health risks from water pollutants:

"Bladder Cancer and Chlorinated Water." *Water Technology*, January 1991.

"Cancer and Chlorinated Water." *Lancet*, 23 May 1981.

Carlo, G. L., and Mettlin, C. J. "Cancer Incidence and Trihalomethane Concentrations in a Public Water Supply." *American Journal of Public Health* 70 (May 1980).

Crawford-Brown, D. J. "Radon in Water." *Water Technology*, May 1991.

League of Women Voters. *Of Mice and Men: Health Risks and Safety Judgements.* Washington, D.C., 1977.

Lowrance, William W. *Of Acceptable Risk.* Los Altos, CA: William Kaufman, Inc., 1976.

National Academy of Sciences. *Principles of Evaluating Chemicals in the Environment.* Washington, D.C., 1975.

National Research Council. *Drinking Water and Health*, Vols. 1–5. Washington, D.C.: National Academic Press, 1977–1983.

Resources for the Future. *Safe Drinking Water: Current and Future Problems.* Report of the National Conference on Drinking Water Policy Problems, Washington, D.C., 1978.

Sterling, C. R. "Cryptosporidium: The Water Industry's New Stomachache." *Water Technology,* July 1990.

Stewart, John Cary. *Drinking Water Hazards.* Hiram, OH: Envirographics, 1990.

On inhalation and skin absorption of pollutants:

Brown, H. S., Bishop, D. R., and Rowan, C. A. "The Role of Skin Absorption as a Route for Exposure to Volatile Organic Compounds in Drinking Water." *American Journal of Public Health*, May 1984.

National Academy of Sciences. *Drinking Water and Health.* Washington, D.C.: NAS/NRC, 1977.

For further information on radon pollution, contact: Environmental Protection Agency, Office of Drinking Water, 401 M Street Southwest, Washington, DC 20460.

On pollution from the distribution system:

Hobil, Johnathan. "Water Supply Issues, Part II: Treatment and Distribution Contamination," *Water Conditioning and Purification,* February 1991.

On fluoridation:

Burk, D. "Fluoridation: A Burning Controversy." *Bestways,* April 1982.

Furman, A. F. "Fluoridation—Boon or Bane." *Health Express,* October 1982.

Waldbott, G. L., et al. *Fluoridation: The Great Dilemma.* Lawrence, KS: Coronado Press, 1978.

Yiamouiannis, J. A. *Everything You Wanted to Know About Fluoridation.* Monrovia, CA: National Health Federation, 1977.

_____. *Lifesavers Guide to Fluoridation: Risks/Benefits.* Delaware, OH: Safe Water Foundation, 1982.

On water testing:

"Affordable Informational Drinking Water Testing." *Water Technology,* May 1990.

"Creating a Market: The Selling of Water Safety." *Consumer Reports,* January 1990.

"Research Team Challenges EPA Bacteria Test." *U.S. Water News,* April 1985.

"Using Water Tests Ethically." *Water Technology,* February 1991.

On health benefits from water:

Crawford, M. D., and Crawford, T. "Mortality and Hardness of Local Water Supplies." *Lancet,* 20 April 1968.

Palmer, David. *Calcium and the Body.* International Water Technologies, Inc., Lincoln, NE.

Robertson, J. S. "Mortality and Hardness of Water." *Lancet,* 1968, no. 2:348.

Winton, E. F. and McCabe, L. J. "Studies Relating to Water Mineralization and Health." *Journal of the American Water Works Association,* January 1970.

On bottled water:

Report on Bottled Water and Bottled Water Substitutes. Suffolk County, NY: Suffolk County Department of Health Services, 1982.

U.S. Congress. House. Committee on Energy and Commerce, Subcommittee on Oversight and Investigations. *Proceedings of the Bottled Water Workshop,* September 13–14, 1990. Washington, D.C.: Government Printing Office, 1990.

APPENDIX C

Water Quality Standards

Definitions For Water Standards

♦ **mg/l** means milligrams of pollutant per liter of water; mg/l is the approximate equivalent of parts per million.

♦ **MCLs** are maximum contaminant levels.

♦ **MCLGs** are maximum contaminant level goals (for the future).

♦ **MFL** is a measure of asbestos and means millions of fibers per liter of water.

♦ **mrem/yr** is a measure of radioactivity received by a person, and stands for millirems per year.

♦ **pCi/l** means picocuries per liter, which is a measure of radioactivity concentration in water.

♦ **Proposed Regulations** are those contaminant limits that have been proposed by the EPA but have not yet become law.

♦ **Secondary Regulations** are nonenforceable, suggested limits on certain water pollutants that impair water's aesthetic qualities.

♦ **turbidity** is the cloudiness of water.

Summary of National Primary Drinking Water Regulations (as of July 1990)

Contaminant	MCLG [1,5]	MCL [1,6]
Microbiological Contaminants		
Coliforms (total)	0	1/100ml[2]
Giardia Lamblia	0	TT[3]
HPC	–	TT[3]
Legionella	0	TT[3]
Virus	0	TT[3]
Turbidity	–	1–5 NTU[4]
Inorganic Contaminants		
Arsenic	–	0.05
Barium	–	1
Cadmium	–	0.010
Chromium	–	0.05
Fluoride	4.0	4.0
Lead	–	0.05
Mercury	–	0.002
Nitrate	–	10
Selenium	–	0.01
Silver	–	0.05
Organic Contaminants		
2,4-D	–	0.1
Endrin	–	0.0002
Lindane	–	0.004
Methoxychlor	–	0.1
2,4,5-TP Silvex	–	0.01
Benzene	0	0.005
Carbon tetrachloride	0	0.005
P-Dichlorobenzene	0.075	0.075
1,2-Dichloroethane	0	0.005
1,1-Dichloroethylene	0.007	0.007
1,1,1-Trichloroethane	0.20	0.20
Trichloroethylene	0	0.005
Vinyl chloride	0	0.002
Total trihalomethanes (Chloroform, Bromoform, Bromodichloromethane, Dibromochloromethane)	–	0.10
Radionuclides		
Gross alpha particle activity	–	15pCi/l
Gross beta particle activity	–	4 mrem/yr.
Radium 226 and 228 (total)	–	5pCi/l

FOOTNOTES FOR THIS CHART APPEAR ON NEXT PAGE

Source: EPA Office of Water

National Secondary Drinking Water Regulations SMCLs*

Contaminant	Level
chloride	250mg/l
color	15 color units
copper	1mg/l
corrosivity	non-corrsive
fluoride	2.0 mg/l
foaming agents	0.5mg/l
iron	0.3 mg/l
manganese	0.05 mg.l
odor	3 threshold odor number
pH	6.5–8.5
sulfate	250 mg/l
total dissoved solids (TDS)	500 mg/l
zinc	5 mg/l

* *Secondary Maximum Contaminant Levels (SMCLs) are federally non-enforceable and establish limits for contaminants in drinking water which may affect the aesthetic qualities and the public's acceptance of drinking water (e.g. taste and odor).*

Proposed Secondary Maximum Contaminant Levels

Contaminant	Level (mg/l)
aluminum	0.05
o-Dichlorobenzene	0.01
p-Dichlorobenzene	0.005
Ethylbenzene	0.03
Pentachlorophenol	0.03
Silver	0.09
Styrene	0.01
Toluene	0.04
Xylene	0.02

FOOTNOTES FOR CHART ON PREVIOUS PAGE—

[1] *In milligrams per liter (mg/l) unless otherwise noted.*

[2] *Revised regulations will be based on presence/absence concept rather than an estimate of coliform density: effective December 1990.*

[3] *TT–Treatment Technique requirements established in lieu of MCLs: effective beginning December 1990.*

[4] *Revised regulations will establish treatment technique requirements rather than an MCL for turbidity: effective beginning December 1990.*

[5] *Maximum contaminant level goal (MCLG) is non-enforceable goal at which no known adverse health effects occur.*

[6] *Maximum contaminant level (MCL) is federally-enforceable standard.*

Source: EPA Office of Water

Proposed National Primary Drinking Water Regulations for Inorganic and Synthetic Organic Contaminants

Contaminant	Proposed MCLG* (mg/l)	Current MCL** (mg/l)	Proposed MCL** (mg/l)
Inorganics			
Asbestos	7 MFL[1]	–	7MFL[1]
Barium	5	1	5
Cadmium	0.005	0.01	0.005
Chromium	0.1	0.05	0.1
Mercury	0.002	0.002	0.002
Nitrate[2]	10	10	10
Nitrite[2]	1	–	1
Selenium	0.05	0.01	0.05
Silver	–	0.05	[3]
VolatileOrganics			
o-Dichlorobenzene	0.6	–	0.6
cis-1,2-Dichloroethylene	0.07	–	0.07
trans-1,2-Dichloropropane	0.1	–	0.1
1,2-Dichloropropane	0	–	0.005
Ethylbenzene	0.7	–	0.7
Nonochlorobenzene	0.1	–	0.1
Styrene	0/0.1	–	0.005/0.1
Tetracholoroethylene	0	–	0.005
Toluene	2	–	2
Xylenes	10	–	10
Pesticides/PCBs			
Alachlor	0	–	0.002
Aldicarb	0.01	–	0.01
Aldicarb sulfoxide	0.01	–	0.01
Aldicarb sulfone	0.04	–	0.04
Atrazine	0.003	–	0.003
Carbofuran	0.04	–	0.04
Chlorodane	0	–	0.0002
2,4-D	0.07	0.1	0.07
Dibromochloropropane	0	–	0.0002
Ethylene dibromide	0	–	0.00005
Heptachlor	0	–	0.0004
Heptachlor epoxide	0	–	0.0002
Lindane	0.0002	0.004	0.0002
Methoxychlor	0.4	0.1	0.4
PCBs	0	–	0.0005
Pentachlorophenol	0.2	–	0.2
Toxaphene	0	0.005	0.005
2,4,5-TP (Silvex)	0.05	0.01	0.05
Water Treatment Chemicals			
Acrylamide	0	–	TT[4]
Epichlorohydrin	0	–	TT[4]

FOOTNOTES FOR THIS CHART APPEAR ON NEXT PAGE

Source: EPA Office of Water

This chart shows proposed maximum contaminant level goals and maximum contaminant levels for 24 additional contaminants, recently announced by EPA. Amounts shown are in milligrams-per-liter.

Contaminant	Proposed MCLG*	Proposed MCL**
Inorganics		
Antimony	0.003	0.01/0.005[1]
Beryllium	0	0.001
Cyanide	0.2	0.2
Nickel	0.1	0.1
Sulfate	400/500[1]	400/500[1]
Thallium	0.0005	0.002/0.001[1]
Organics		
Dalapon	0.2	0.2
Dichloromethane	0	0.005
Dinoseb	0.007	0.007
Diquat	0.02	0.02
Di(ethylhexyl)adipate	0.5	0.5
Di(ethylexyl)phthalate	0	0.004
Endothall	0.1	0.1
Endrin	0.002	0.002
Glyphosate	0.7	0.7
Hexachlorobenzene	0	0.001
Hexachlorocyclopentadiene	0.05	0.05
Oxymyl (Vydate)	0.2	0.2
PAHs[2] (Benzo(a)pyrene)	0	0.0002
Picloram	0.5	0.5
Simazine	0.001	0.001
1,2,4-Trichlorobenzene	0.009	0.009
1,1,2-Trichloroethane	0.003	0.005
2,3,7,8-TCDD (dioxin)	0	5×10^{-8}

* *Maximum Contaminant Level Goal, a non-enforceable health protection goal*
** *Maximum Contaminant Level, a federally-enforceable standard*
[1] *EPA is considering alternative MCLGs and/or MCLs for these inorganics. After public comment, a single MCLG and MCL will be set.*
[2] *TT=in addition to benzo(a)pyrene, EPA his considering establishing an MCLG and an MCL for six additional polynuclear aromatic hydrocarbons (PAHs) classified as probable human carcinogens.*

FOOTNOTES FOR CHART ON PREVIOUS PAGE—

* *Maximum Contaminant Level Goal, a non-enforceable health protection goal*
** *Maximum Contaminant Level, a federally-enforceable standard*
[1] *MFL=Million Fibers per Liter longer than 10 μm*
[2] *The MCLG and MCL for total nitrate and nitrite is 10 mg/l (as N)*
[3] *Deleted as primary regulation; proposed as secondary*
[4] *TT=treatment technique requirement*

Source: EPA Office of Water

APPENDIX D

Water Testing Information

The following automated laboratories offer (relatively) low-cost, comprehensive water tests.

> National Testing Laboratories, Inc.
> 6151 Wilson Mills Road
> Cleveland, OH 44143
> (800) 458-3330

Tests included in the "Watercheck" series (cost, $89):

METALS:
- Arsenic
- Barium
- Cadmium
- Chromium
- Copper
- Iron
- Lead
- Manganese
- Mercury
- Nickel
- Selenium
- Silver
- Sodium
- Zinc

INORGANICS AND PHYSICAL FACTORS:
- Total alkalinity
- Chloride
- Fluoride
- Nitrate
- Nitrite
- Sulfate

- Hardness
- pH
- Total dissolved solids
- Turbidity

VOLATILE ORGANICS:
- Bromoform
- Bromodichloromethane
- Chloroform
- Dibromochloromethane
- Total trihalomethanes
- Benzene
- Vinyl chloride
- Carbon tetrachloride
- 1,2-Dichloroethane
- Trichloroethylene
- 1,4-Dichlorobenzene
- 1,1-Dichloroethylene
- 1,1,1-Trichloroethane
- Bromobenzene
- Bromomethane
- Chlorobenzene
- Chloroethane
- Chloromethane

- O-Chlorotoluene
- P-Chlorotoluene
- Dibromochloropropane
- Dibromomethane
- 1,2-Dichlorobenzene
- 1,3-Dichlorobenzene
- trans-1,2-Dichloroethylene
- cis-1,2-Dichloroethylene
- Dichloromethane
- 1,1-Dichloroethane
- 1,1-Dichloropropene
- 1,2-Dichloropropane
- trans-1,3-Dichloropropene
- cis-1,3-Dichloropropene
- 2,2-Dichloropropane
- Ethylene dibromide
- Ethylbenezene

- Styrene
- 1,1,2-Trichloroethane
- 1,1,1,2-Tetrachloroethane
- 1,1,2,2,-Tetrachloroethane
- Tetrachloroethylene
- 1,2,3-Trichloropropane
- Toluene
- Xylene
- Chloroethylvinyl ether
- Dichlorodifluoromethane
- 1,3-Dichloropropane
- Trichlorofluoromethane
- Trichlorobenzene(s)

MICROBIOLOGICAL:
- Coliform bacteria

Tests included in the pesticide option (add $30 to above):

**ORGANIC CHEMICALS—PESTICIDES—
HERBICIDES AND PCBs**
- Alachlor
- Aldrin
- Atrazine
- Chlordane
- Dichloran
- Dieldren
- Endrin
- Heptachlor
- heptachlor epoxide
- Hexachlorobenzene

- Hexachloropentadiene
- Lindane
- Methoxychlor
- PCBs
- Pentachloronitrobenzene
- Silvex 1,4,5-TP
- Simazine
- Toxaphene
- Trifluralin
- 2,4-D

Comments: The above is, at this writing, the best buy of any tests offered. Important pollutants not included are asbestos and radon.

Spectrum Labs, Inc.
301 West County Road
New Brighton, MN 55112
(612) 633-0101

Tests included in the "Drinking Water and Organics" series (cost, $88):

- Visual inspection
- Total hardness
- Sodium
- Iron
- Manganese
- Copper
- pH
- Total dissolved solids (by conductivity)
- Total alkalinity
- Chloride
- Sulfate
- Fluoride
- Nitrate
- Lead
- Total trihalomethanes
- Chloroform
- Bromoform
- Dibromochloromethane
- Bromodichloromethane
- 1,2-Dichloroethane
- Benzene
- Toluene
- Chlorobenzene
- Ethylbenzene
- Methylene chloride
- Trichlorofluoromethane
- 1,1-Dichloroethylene
- 1,1-Dichloroethane
- trans-1,2-Dichloroethylene
- 1,1,1-Trichloroethane
- Carbon tetrachloride
- 1,2-Dichloropropane
- trans-1,3-Dichloropropene
- Trichloroethylene
- 1,1,2-Trichloroethane
- cis-1,3-Dichloropropene
- 2-Choroethyl Vinyl Ether
- Tetrachloroethylene
- 1,1,2,2-Tetrachloroethane

Tests included in the "Heavy Metals" series (cost, $73)

- Arsenic
- Barium
- Cadmium
- Chromium
- Copper
- Iron
- Lead
- Manganese
- Silver

Tests included in the "FHA Analysis" series (cost, $29)

- Coliform bacteria and nitrates

Comments on the above tests: Still a pretty good bargain. Important pollutants not included are asbestos and radon.

Home Test
33 South Commercial Street
Manchester, NH 03108
(800) 253-3506

Tests included in the "Toxic Metals" series (cost, $20):

- Arsenic
- Barium
- Cadmium
- Nickel
- Copper
- Iron
- Lead
- Manganese
- Magnesium
- Calcium
- Chromium
- Sodium
- Zinc

Tests included in the "Comprehensive Test" series (cost, $50):

- Arsenic
- Barium
- Cadmium
- Calcium
- Corrosivity
- Specific conductance
- Nitrate
- Lead
- Manganese
- Magnesium
- Nickel
- Chromium
- Copper
- Coliform/fecal bacteria
- Fluoride
- Alkalinity
- Chloride
- Hardness
- Sodium
- Zinc
- Iron

Tests included in the "Pesticides" series (cost, $45):

- Atrazine
- Alachlor
- Aldrin
- Chlordane
- Dieldrin
- Endrin
- Heptachlor
- Heptachlor epoxide
- Hexachlorobenzene
- Lindane
- Methoxychlor
- Toxaphene

Tests included in the "Organic Compounds" series (cost, $45)

- Chloroform
- Bromodichloromethane
- Dibromochloromethane
- Bromoform
- Benzene
- Bromobenzene
- Bromomethane
- n-Butylbenzene
- sec-Butylbenzene
- tert-Butylbenzene
- Carbon Tetrachloride
- Chlorobenzene
- Chloromethane
- 2-Chlorotoluene
- 4-Chlorotoluene
- 1,2-Dibromo-3-chloropropane
- 1,2-Dibromoethane
- Dibromomethane
- 1,2-Dichlorobenzene
- 1,3-Dichlorobenzene
- 1,4-Dichlorobenzene
- 1,1-Dichloroethane
- 1,2-Dichloroethane
- 1,1-Dichloroethylene
- trans-1,2-Dichloroethylene
- cis-1,2-Dichloroethylene
- 1,2-Dichloropropane
- 1,3-Dichloropropane
- 2,2-Dichloropropane
- 1,1-Dichloropropene
- Ethylbenzene
- Hexachlorobutadiene
- Isopropylbenzene
- p-Isopropyltoluene
- Methylene Chloride
- Napthalene
- n-Propylbenzene
- Styrene
- 1,1,1,2-Tetrachloroethane
- 1,1,2,2-Tetrachloroethane
- Tetrachloroethylene
- Toluene
- 1,2,3-Trichlorobenzene
- 1,2,4-Trichlorobenzene
- 1,1,1-Trichloroethane
- Trichloroethylene
- Trichlorofluoromethane
- 1,2,3-Trichloropropane
- 1,2,4-Trimethylbenzene
- 1,3,5-Trimethylbenzene
- o-Xylene
- m,p-Xylenes
- cis-1,3-Dichloropropane
- trans-1,3-Dichloropropene

Radon tests are available from $30 to $55.

Comments on the above tests: Good bargains and good quality. Asbestos test not available.

Asbestos testing in water is not commonly available. It is also inconclusive because asbestos concentrations in water can fluctuate abruptly and dramatically. To find out more about asbestos testing, contact the Environmental Protection Agency (see Appendix B) or your state environmental health department.

APPENDIX E

Certified Water Bottlers

As of this writing, the following brands of bottled water have been certified by the Food and Drug Administration as meeting the Title 21 Code of Federal Regulations, Chapter 1, Parts 103, 110 and 129.

Trade Name	Trade Name
Abita	Midas
Alhambra	Mississippi
AquaPenn	Mount Olympus
Aspen	Mountain Valley
Clearbrook	Ozarka
Cloister	Publix
Crystal	Pure Mountain
Crystal Rock	Puro
Culligan	Roaring Spring
Deep Rock	Sapphire Mountain
Deer Park	Shamrock
Ephrata	Snow Valley
Eureka	Sparkletts
Georgia Mountain	Springlite
Kentwood	Triple Springs
Keystone	Triton
Land O Sky	Utopia
Leisure Time	

Colin Ingram's Water Quality Experience

Colin Ingram has thirty years' experience as a scientific writer, researcher, and technical publishing consultant to universities, corporations, and government agencies. He has published more than three hundred books, manuals, and reports on scientific and technical subjects. From 1982 through 1987, he conducted a five-year research program on all aspects of drinking water, including health risk assessment, regional mapping of water quality, a bottled water study, an evaluation of water testing laboratories in the United States, and extensive water purification product evalution and testing. His other water publications include *Consumers' Guide to Safe Drinking Water* (1985), *Water Contamination—A National Problem* (1987), and *A Survey of Water Purification Problems and Product Recommendations for Private Water Systems* (1987).

Books for your lifestyle

YOUR HOME, YOUR HEALTH, AND WELL-BEING
by David Rousseau, W.J. Rea, M.D. and Jean Enwright

" A well-illustrated, thoroughly researched look at home pollutants and how to transform your living space into a more healthful one." —*East West Magazine*

A guide to the many substances in modern homes which can cause irritation, stress, allergies, even severe environmental illness—and what you can do about them. An indispensable resource for homeowners, renters, architects, builders, and landscapers. $14.95 paper, 320 pages

HEALING ENVIRONMENTS
by Carol Venolia

This holistic approach to "indoor well-being" examines healing, awareness, and empowerment, and how they are affected by various aspects of our environment. Its principles can be applied to homes, workplaces, and healthcare centers to bring greater peace and harmony into our lives. $9.95 paper, 224 pages
A Celestial Arts Book

COHOUSING
by Kathryn McCamant and Charles Durrett

"Enthusiastic . . . filled with lovely photographs, architectural renderings, and detailed advice . . . Many readers will want to explore it for alternative choices."

—*Los Angeles Times*

Cohousing is an exciting new approach to housing which is taking Europe by storm, and gaining popularity in the U.S. It allows residents to develop specialized communities which combine the autonomy of private homes with the advantages of shared facilities. $21.95 paper, 208 pages

ALTERNATIVE ENERGY SOURCEBOOK
by The Real Goods Company

The most complete resource book available for people who want to develop alternative energy sources, this compendium lists hundreds of products and ideas that range from cutting-edge, revolutionary new technologies to simple, time-tested ideas. Profusely illustrated with photos and diagrams. $16.00 paper, 400 pages

Available from your local bookstore, or order direct from the publisher. Please include $1.25 shipping & handling for the first book, and 50¢ for each additional book. California residents include local sales tax. Write for our free complete catalog of over 400 books and tapes.

TEN SPEED PRESS
P. O. Box 7123   Berkeley, California 94707
(510) 845-8414